Meet Me
on the
Mountain

William J. Petersen

While this book is designed for the reader's personal enjoyment and profit, it is also intended for group study. A Leader's Guide with Victor Multiuse Transparency Masters is available from your local bookstore or from the publisher at $2.25.

VICTOR BOOKS

a division of SP Publications, Inc., Wheaton, Illinois
Offices also in Fullerton, California • Whitby, Ontario, Canada • London, England

Recommended Dewey Decimal Classification: 221.924
    Suggested Subject Headings: OLD TESTAMENT—BIOGRAPHY
Library of Congress Catalog Card Number: 78-68861
ISBN: 0-88207-784-8

VICTOR BOOKS
A division of SP Publications, Inc.
P.O. Box 1825 • Wheaton, Illinois 60187

Contents

Like Me?

1

James 5:17

I had a hard time identifying with Elijah. And that was the problem. I was supposed to be able to identify with him. The Bible said so.

You remember Elijah, don't you? That Old Testament blood-and-guts prophet who stood jaw to jaw with wicked King Ahab and told him that it wouldn't rain in his kingdom for three years.

You remember Elijah. That intrepid man of faith who prayed to God for a boy who had died and the boy was restored to life again.

You remember Elijah. That fearless defender of God's truth who challenged 450 prophets of Baal to a fire-from-heaven contest on top of Mount Carmel and then lopped off their heads in his victory celebration. How could any normal human being living in the 20th century possibly identify with a man like that?

It was a little phrase that James wrote to the Hebrew Christians that got to me. "Elijah was a man subject to like passions as we are" (James 5:17, KJV).

Evidently James was saying that Elijah had a lot in common with me. And with you.

I had a hard time thinking of Elijah, waiting on the corner with me for the commuter bus to the city, or buying hamburgers for the family at McDonald's on Saturday night.

I couldn't see why James didn't ask me to identify with Peter. Now there's a guy who was a little bit of Everyman. He was always putting his foot in his mouth, which is about as universal a trait as there is. He made New Year's resolutions that were broken before the Rose Bowl Parade was finished. And when the crunch came, Peter denied the Lord. Any time I hear a message on the life of Peter, I always say, "That's me!"

Or how about David? You can empathize with David in his Psalms. At times he didn't seem to comprehend what God was doing. He had problems with his children; he didn't know whom he could trust; and of course, you know about his affair with Bathsheba. Yes, David was certainly "a man of like passions as we are."

But whether I liked it or not, James didn't mention either Peter or David; instead, he called that desert-dwelling, shaggy-haired Elijah "a man of like passions as we are."

A Man Just Like Us

What does that really mean, "a man of like passions"? Our use of the word *passion* might lead us to think that he made it a practice to stand outside the local apothecary shop in downtown Jericho and ogle the maidens who happened to pass by. Or that he couldn't pass up a banana split or a piece of strawberry shortcake.

I checked my other Bible versions, which I keep on my bookshelf for such occasions as this. How did they translate "a man of like passions"? Here's what I found:

"Elijah was a man with a nature like ours" (NASB).

"Elijah was a human being with a nature such as we have—with feelings, affections and constitution as ourselves" (AMP).

"Elijah was a man just like us" (NIV).

"Elijah was a man with feelings just like ours" (WMS).

"He was a man as human as we are" (PH).

As I studied the passage in James more thoroughly, I saw that he was saying that Elijah was a normal human being and that God miraculously answered his prayers.

In the first century, when James lived, there were many popular legends about Elijah. He was regarded as Daniel Boone, Robin Hood, and Superman all wrapped up in one. When James used Elijah as his example of effective praying, he wanted his readers to understand that Elijah was "a man just like us."

In fact, the Greek word James used to describe Elijah is used only one other time in the Bible. On Paul's first missionary journey, as recorded in the Book of Acts, things were going from bad to worse for Paul and Barnabas until they hit the town of Lystra in the hills of central Asia Minor. A crippled man was healed, and the two missionaries found themselves to be instant celebrities. The townsfolk thought they must be two Greek gods who had dropped in out of the blue. They called Barnabas Jupiter, and Paul Mercury, and were preparing to sacrifice some oxen to them. After he finally got their attention, Paul said, "Why are you doing this? We also are men, of like nature with you" (Acts 14:15, RSV). In other words, "We're men just like you."

The Greek word very literally means "of like feelings." *Homo* means "like," as in a homogeneous class. And *pathos* means "feeling," as in sympathy or empathy.

All of which didn't help me emphathize with Elijah. How could I put myself in Elijah's shoes, or more accurately, in his sandals?

I resolved to take another look at Elijah, to reread those familiar stories that I had heard since I was a child in Sunday School. This time, as I read them, I would put myself in Elijah's place. I would feel how his heart would pound and his knees would knock as he approached Ahab's chariot; I would enter into the loneliness after that mountaintop experience on Mount Carmel; I would try to understand what it must have been like to be fed by ravens at Brook Cherith.

An Ordinary Man

God uses ordinary people; and Elijah was an ordinary man. Harold W. Fife in his study on Elijah, *A Man Just like Us* (Christian Literature Crusade), says, "The real difference between Ahab and Elijah was not in their passion but in the outlets for it. Ahab, incited by Jezebel, allowed it to ride him into appalling idolatry and unspeakable sin. Elijah, incited by the Spirit, allowed it to drive him to passionate prayer. It is not our passions that make or break us; it is the way they are channeled."

It is as we identify with the characters in the Bible that we can fully appropriate the truths that they would teach us. If we place them on pedestals and put halos on them, we will not learn from them.

However, when I read what some of the great theologians and preachers of the past said about Elijah, I did feel some awe.

Bishop Hall, a 17th-century churchman, said, "He was the eminentest prophet reserved for the corruptest age." Hall must have been smitten by superlatives. Two centuries later, the Scottish-born clergyman John Cunningham Geikie called him "the grandest and most romantic character that Israel ever produced." More superlatives. And to top it off, the British preacher F. B. Meyer referred to Elijah as "this Colossus among ordinary men, who dwarfs us while his own noble proportions defy the belittling perspective of long distance."

Far be it from me to contradict F. B. Meyer, but if James can refer to Elijah as a man of like passions as we are, so can I. And that's what we're going to do in this book.

The Man Himself

Before we take a look at Elijah in action, let's move in for a close-up of the man himself.

If Elijah's name were to appear in the *Who's Who in Israel* of his day, using only the information we have about him, the entry might look like this:

ELIJAH: (born about 900 B.C.) Parents unknown. *Hometown:* probably Tishbe in the province of Gilead, or maybe Tishbe in the province of Naphtali. *Education:* Unknown. *Occupation:* Part-time prophet. *Residences:* Tishbe (?); Brook Cherith; Zarephath, Phoenicia; Mount Sinai. *Major accomplishments:* Predicted three-year drought in Israel during King Ahab's reign; defeated prophets of Baal on Mount Carmel; reactivated school for prophets; selected Elisha as his successor. *Death:* surrounded in mystery.

The surprising thing is not what you know about Elijah, but how much you don't know.

Most of the other Old Testament prophets tell you at least who their parents are. There was Isaiah, son of Amoz; Jeremiah, son of Hilkiah; Ezekiel, son of Buzi; Hosea, son of Beeri; and so on.

And sometimes you know their occupation for profit, when they weren't busy in their prophet occupation. Amos was a herdsman; Jeremiah and Ezekiel were priests.

But Elijah is a mystery man. You don't know his parents; you don't know his occupation; even his hometown is debatable. When he suddenly comes on the scene in 1 Kings 18:1, he is identified as Elijah the Tishbite from the land of Gilead, and most scholars think that this means he came from some place called Tishbe, Gilead. But they've never been able to pinpoint Tishbe on a Gilead roadmap. However, there was a Tishbe in the province of Naphtali, so it's possible that he was born in Tishbe, Naphtali, and moved to Gilead at an early age; and then there's a third possibility. Since *Tishbe* really means "sojourner," maybe the verse should simply be translated "a sojourner in the land of Gilead."

The fact is that Gilead was on the other side of the Jordan River from the main part of Israel. It was rural and mountainous, and you could pass through most of Gilead's major metropolitan centers—and certainly Tishbe—without knowing you had come into town. Most Israelites regarded Gilead in the same way that Americans a century ago regarded the Rocky Mountain States. In Arabic, the name *Gilead* means "rough and rugged," and you can't describe the area better than that.

Today, Gilead forms the heart of the rather barren nation of Jordan, but 2,800 years ago there were forests on those limestone hills instead of the occasional scrub oak you see today. In fact, the forests of Gilead were almost as famous as the forests of Lebanon, and the balm of Gilead, derived from the gum of a small tree in those forests, became world renowned.

Where the Jabbok Valley cuts through the dolomite limestone into the sandstone cliffs, steep ravines and gorges were formed. Red and white oleander flowers fringed the cascading streams. On the lowland, tamarisk and lotus grew.

Like the American Rockies, Gilead's highlands rose abruptly and then settled into plateaus which gradually degenerated into endless deserts. On the one side were precipitous ravines, streams, and springs; on the other, a white chalky desert.

To Elijah, Gilead was home. Its residents were simple, independent people. They were frontiersmen, guarding the eastern flank of Israel from desert marauders. According to Geikie, it was "a land of tent villages and mountain castles; with a population of wandering, half-civilized, fierce shepherds, ready at all times to repel the attacks of the desert tribes, or to go out on a foray against them."

You can almost imagine Elijah as a boy leaping across a deep ravine, climbing a mountainside, clinging to slippery ledges, running fleet-footed down a dry streambed. He was an outdoorsman, through and through.

A predecessor of the modern Bedouins, Elijah was, according to the biblical clues, a hardy long-distance runner, swarthy in complexion and abrupt in manner. Like today's marathon competitor, he raced from the slopes of Mount Carmel to Ahab's royal city and beat the king's chariot. You have the feeling that Elijah was a solitary man, thrust into prominence he really didn't enjoy.

Elijah still doesn't sound like your next-door neighbor, does he? And he didn't look like him either.

According to Jewish tradition, his hair was long and thick. His clothing consisted of a simple tunic, which he would tie around him with a wide belt. In the cool mountain air or in the face of a treacherous sandstorm from the east, he wore a camel's hair mantle or cloak.

Jehovah Is God

How can you identify with Elijah? And why does the Bible suggest that Elijah could identify with your feelings?

Well, first of all, his name may give a clue. *Elijah* is composed of two Hebrew names for God, *El* and *Jah*; literally it means "Jehovah is God." Now that may sound like double-talk, but it really isn't.

You see, the first big slip of Elijah's regal foe, Ahab, was not an outright denial of Jehovah. He didn't say that Jehovah wasn't a god. He merely said that Jehovah wasn't the only god.

When he married Jezebel, Ahab thought it the gentlemanly thing to do to give equal time to Baal. It seemed rather narrow-minded to say that Jehovah was the one and only deity, especially when his queen came from a foreign country that worshiped another god. Ahab even had prophets of Jehovah in his temple and he called his children by names of Jehovah. Maybe Ahab doesn't deserve the bad press he has gotten for nearly 3,000 years.

To play it safe, his citizens followed suit. If one God

was good, two gods must be even better. So they adopted Baal-worship as a second religion. If they could placate both gods, they wouldn't suffer from the wrath of either. Or so they thought.

But at his summit conference on Mount Carmel, Elijah called out: "How long will you hesitate between two opinions? If the Lord is God, follow Him; but if Baal, follow him" (1 Kings 18:21).

And when Elijah said, "If the Lord (Jehovah) is God," he was practically saying his own name.

In other words, you can't serve both Jehovah and Baal. This kind of exclusivism is no more popular today than it was in the days of Elijah, but the message of Elijah is still needed.

By his very name, Elijah showed his true colors. No wonder Queen Jezebel didn't like to hear about the man from Gilead. As a Baal-worshiper, she recoiled in anger every time someone said, "Here comes old 'Jehovah is God.'" If he had had another name, he might not have been as much of a problem to her. She might get away from Elijah but she never could get away from his name. Someone was always talking about "Jehovah-is-God." Little wonder she developed a paranoiac reaction to him.

His name was his bumper sticker. Even when he was moping on Mount Sinai, his name was a reminder of the sovereignty of Jehovah. He could never forget the significance of his name.

If you bear the name *Christian*, you believe that Jesus is the way, the truth, and the life, and that no one comes to the Father but through Him. Normally, of course, people don't mind what religion you follow. You can practice levitation in your living room or have a shrine to the "Destroyer-god" Shiva in your backyard, and your neighbors won't care. The rub comes when you as a Christian seek to share your faith and say that Jesus is the only way.

Like Elijah, you live in a pluralistic society, a society which believes that there are many options open to a person who wants to develop spiritually. Choosing a religion is pretty much like buying a car. You pick one you like in order to meet the needs of the moment. Maybe when you're in your twenties you're in the mood for a sports car; in your thirties you might opt for a station wagon; in your forties you might start to become more conservative and traditional in your tastes. Just so, our society says that you pick religion to meet the needs of the moment; and any religion, if it meets your needs, is valid.

But there is something related to faith which is even more subtle, more insidious. It's one thing to declare that Jehovah, not Baal, is God. That notion may not be popular in society, but at least you know where you stand.

But when Jesus said, "You cannot serve God and Mammon," (Matt. 6:24) He wasn't talking about a heathen god. It sounded like Elijah saying, "You can't serve God and Baal," but the choices were different. Jesus wasn't talking about a pagan deity; He was talking about materialism, about a success-oriented society. And that gets embarrassingly close to home.

Mankind has had a long-standing attachment to money and property. Unfortunately, many Christian men and women live a value system very much like that of their world. While professing Christ, they live with Mammon.

That's why you need to identify with Elijah in his name, "Jehovah is God." God must be sovereign over all your interests, entertainments, and pleasures; He must be sovereign over your vocation and avocation;

He must be sovereign over the way you make and spend your money.

Learn to Be Human

How did Elijah learn that Jehovah was truly Lord of all? There are Bible teachers who suggest that Elijah stepped out of the badlands of Gilead as an instant saint. But I doubt it. Abraham, Moses, and David weren't instant saints when God started working with them. And I don't think Elijah was either.

It's possible, though, that he thought he was. But God knew better. So God provided some very extraordinary learning experiences in some most unusual classrooms.

One of the things that God was teaching Elijah was identification. All through his life Elijah was learning how to be "a man of like passions as we are."

Does that sound odd? Do we have to learn to be human? Some of us do. Some of us have a harder time relating to people than we have in relating to things. And this is an important lesson to learn because if we find it difficult to relate to people, we may find it difficult to relate to God in a warm and personal way.

When Jesus said, "Blessed are the merciful, for they shall receive mercy" (Matt. 5:7), He was implying something about the importance of identifying with others.

Sometimes we tend to think of mercy as a negative quality. I once heard it defined this way: "Grace is God's giving us what we don't deserve; mercy is God's not giving us what we do deserve." In other words, grace gives us heaven; mercy keeps us from hell. But that is not the meaning of mercy, particularly in the Old Testament understanding of the word.

In a commentary on the Gospel of Matthew, one

writer speaks of mercy as the special characteristic of God in His relationship with men.

As he explores the Hebrew word for mercy, this commentator says that it is "the ability to get right inside the other person's skin until we can see things with his eyes, think things with his mind, and feel things with his feelings. . . . It denotes a sympathy which is not given, as it were, from outside, but which comes from a deliberate identification with the other person, until we see things as he sees them and feel things as he feels them."

Now that's a difficult virtue for anyone to cultivate. When we sympathize, we usually sympathize from the outside. We seldom get into another person's shoes and truly empathize.

The Bible says that Elijah became like us in our feelings. But the word *mercy* goes beyond identification. It really means "identifying so completely with another person that you do something to meet his need." Of course, the beauty of all this for us is that in Jesus Christ, God literally entered into our skin; He felt things as we feel them. "Surely He hath borne our griefs and carried our sorrows," said Isaiah (Isa. 53:4). He is not a God who "cannot sympathize with our weaknesses, but One who has been tempted in all things as we are, yet without sin" (Heb. 4:15). That's identification. And then Jesus did something to meet our need.

"While we were yet sinners, Christ died for us" (Rom. 5:8). God caused Christ "who knew no sin to be sin on our behalf, that we might become the righteousness of God in Him" (2 Cor. 5:21). He identified with us completely to completely meet our need.

By nature, Elijah was not a merciful man, but God was working *with* Elijah at the same time that He was working *through* him. And that's what makes the life of Elijah such a profitable and fascinating exploration.

I had never before thought that the verse, "Blessed are the merciful" (Matt. 5:7), should be applied to Elijah. But if identification and involvement are keys to being merciful, Elijah is Exhibit A.

What a Way to Go!

2 2 Kings 1:1—2:11

Long before Elijah walked the land of Israel, a shepherd named Moses came one day to Mount Horeb, the mountain of God. There God appeared to him, and gave him a commission to go back to Egypt and lead His people to freedom.

After some discussion, Moses said, "What if they will not believe me, or listen to what I say? For they may say, 'The Lord has not appeared to you.'"

And the Lord said to him, "What is that in your hand?" and he said, "A staff" (see Ex. 3—4).

God was using a simple thing like a shepherd's staff to represent the spiritual reality that He can use whatever a person has and brings to Him. Even in a case like Elijah's.

Of course, compared to Elijah, Moses had a great deal going for him. Although God spoke to him from a burning bush while he was tending sheep in the desert, Moses had been raised in Pharaoh's court. As the adopted son of Pharaoh's daughter, he had leadership training that was fitting for a prince in

Egypt. God was going to use that training to lead His chosen people.

Or think of Joseph for a moment. He had a noble heritage. His great-grandfather was Abraham. His grandfather was Isaac. His father was Jacob, Israel, a Prince with God. And when Joseph was sold and taken to Egypt, he became the manager of affairs of one of Pharaoh's chief officers. All of that prepared him for his future as Egypt's prime minister.

Who Was Elijah?

But Elijah? What did he have? In his hand or in his background? Elijah was from the wrong side of the river, from hillbilly country. Besides that, he didn't have a family tree to talk about, or education or training that would propel him into prominence and responsibility.

ELIJAH: God, I don't know what I have that You can use.

GOD: Well, Elijah, you believe Me, don't you?

ELIJAH: Yes, I believe You, Lord.

GOD: I can use that.

ELIJAH: How?

GOD: Faith can move mountains, you know.

ELIJAH: I didn't say I had faith.

GOD: But you said you believed Me.

ELIJAH: Yes.

GOD: That's faith, Elijah. Let's start from there.

ELIJAH: Well, all right, if You want to call it faith, call it faith. But I sure didn't move any mountains in Gilead.

GOD: I can do great and mighty things through you. Take it from Me, Elijah. The biggest mountain in Israel will never be the same after you and I get through with it.

Elijah the Tishbite

Of course, that's not quite the way the Bible tells the story. Elijah burst upon the scene, without introduction. In 1 Kings 17:1, he is simply called Elijah the Tishbite. Not Elijah the prophet or Elijah the seer. In the Old Testament, whenever an established prophet is introduced, he is called a prophet. Elijah, however, is simply called a Tishbite.

Most of Jehovah's prophets had already been slain by Queen Jezebel, according to 1 Kings 18:4, where we read that Obadiah was able to keep 100 prophets cloistered in a cave. If Elijah had been recognized as a prophet, he would have been lodging in Obadiah's cave, or running from Jezebel's sword.

Most people, when they start to tell the story of Elijah, begin with the first verse of 1 Kings 17, because that's where Elijah's name is first used in the Bible. But verse 1 begins with the word "And," and that indicates that the verse is related to the events of the preceding chapter. So let's take a look at the background.

About 125 years before Elijah, in the year 1,000 B.C., Israel was in its heyday, both spiritually and politically. David, a military king, had stretched the borders of Israel far to the north and the south. Because the Egyptian Empire was in a state of decline and because the Assyrian Empire was still in an embryo state, Israel was, for a short time, one of the most powerful and influential nations in the world. After David, Solomon took over the reins of government. He erected his magnificent temple, established a strong navy, controlled trade routes to India and Africa and devoted himself to farsighted public works projects.

But after Solomon, things fell apart. The Israeli

kingdom was rent asunder. Ten of the 12 tribes of Israel seceded from the Union. Their leader, Jeroboam, installed calf worship as the official religion of his Northern Kingdom. It wasn't that he had anything against Jehovah; it was simply that Jehovah's temple was in the Southern Kingdom of Judah and he thought it politically unwise to encourage his citizens to trek to Jerusalem for their periodic feasts.

To Jeroboam, good politics had a higher priority than good religion. And the bitter fruit of that policy was seen in what happened to the heirs to the throne.

1. Jeroboam's son was Nadab. He lasted only two years on the throne before he was assassinated by Baasha, who, just to be on the safe side, killed the rest of Jeroboam's family. That eliminated all rivals to the throne.

2. Baasha intended to start a new dynasty, and though he managed to survive 24 years as king, his reign was inglorious, and his dynasty was short-lived.

3. Baasha's son was Elah, a worthless carouser. He survived two years as king before he was slain while in a drunken stupor by one of his military leaders. The assassin, Zimri by name, promptly massacred all of Elah's relatives and friends. Sound familiar?

4. Of course, Zimri proclaimed himself as the new king. He hardly had time to have the crown fitted to his head when another military leader marched against him. So Zimri dashed into his palace (I guess you could say it was his), and set it afire, so no one else would have the privilege of living in it. In the blaze, Zimri himself was cremated; thus ended his reign of seven short days.

5. The military leader who fomented the rebellion against Zimri was Omri, and after a bloody civil war, Omri took undisputed possession of the throne. And

the Bible says that Omri "acted more wickedly than all who were before him" (1 Kings 16:25), if you can imagine how that could be.

Omri wasn't good, but he was shrewd. Since Zimri had burned down the previous palace, Omri took advantage of the opportunity to move the capital of Israel to Samaria (16:24), which was strategically more defensible, and built an ivory palace there. Because of his ivory palace and his shrewd foreign relations, archeologists have dug up a good bit of information on Omri.

No doubt, Omri had a hand in arranging the marriage of his son Ahab to Princess Jezebel of Sidon. It seemed to be the wisest move politically. (Politics before religion, remember?) After all, Israel had been having trouble with Syria to the north and Assyria to the northeast. Having his son marry Jezebel of Sidon would insure good relations with the Phoenicians in the west. And that was not only good politics but it was also good business because it opened up trade routes to the Mediterranean.

6. Of course, Omri's son Ahab soon became king. And while the Bible says that Omri was more evil than all his predecessors, it states that Ahab "did more to provoke the Lord God of Israel than all the kings of Israel who were before him" (16:33).

No one knows if Ahab would have deserved that ignominious distinction without the help of Jezebel. Queen Jezebel was a zealous worshiper of the Phoenician deity Baal, but she was not content to conduct her worship privately. She insisted on imposing this immoral religion on the citizenry of Israel. As a dutiful husband, Ahab built a temple and an altar to Baal in the capital city of Samaria. That's when the story of Elijah begins.

God Does the Unlikely

If you were a God-fearing Israelite living in the reign of Ahab, you would probably be asking, "How long, Lord? Why don't You do something about this mess? Why don't You send us a deliverer like Moses or a prophet like Samuel? Or have You forgotten us?"

In every period of history there have been men and women who have agonized in prayer before God regarding the sins of their nation. In every age there are those who are so burdened with the injustice of society and the hurts inflicted upon God's people that they can't understand God's seeming inactivity.

But God is not sleeping, nor is He uncaring. Soon an Elijah will burst upon the scene out of nowhere. He may appear to be an unlikely choice to confront Ahab; he may seem to possess none of the attributes needed to be a leader of God's people. But God delights in using the unlikely.

Remember Gideon? An angel came to this farm boy with the words, "The Lord is with you, O valiant warrior" (Jud. 6:12). Gideon must have thought the angel was knocking on the wrong door. God delights in using the unlikely and doing the unexpected.

Hiel's Story

Between God's candid description of wicked King Ahab (16:33) and the introduction of Elijah (17:1), there is a single verse inserted that most people overlook, 16:34, which tells a story all by itself. In a way, it seems parenthetical, as if the writer of 1 Kings had an extra bit of information and didn't know where else to put it.

This single verse tells the story of Hiel, a native of Bethel, who started a building development in Jericho. Two of his sons died, apparently in the construction work. And the Bible indicates that this happened in fulfillment of the prophecy Joshua had made many years earlier.

What was that prediction? After the walls of that city of Jericho had miraculously fallen down, Joshua, the commanding general of the Israelite forces, said, "Cursed before the Lord is the man who rises up and builds this city Jericho; with the loss of his firstborn he shall lay its foundation, and with the loss of his youngest son he shall set up its gates" (Josh. 6:26).

Hundreds of years had passed since Joshua had cursed the city. Most people had forgotten about it. In fact, most citizens of the Northern Kingdom of Israel couldn't remember anything God had done.

To Hiel, the building contractor, Jericho was an ideal location for a suburban development. Because it lay in the Jordan Valley, halfway between the hills of Samaria and the hills of Gilead, it made an ideal winter resort. As a land developer, Hiel was smart. But as a student of Scripture, he was ignorant. And through his disregard of God's Word, his two sons perished.

Then Elijah walked into the spotlight. The old Jewish rabbis had a brief commentary in the Talmud that said that Ahab and Elijah first met in Jericho at the funeral for Hiel's sons.

That makes sense. King Ahab would have been interested in rebuilding Jericho because it would mean a settlement on his eastern frontier. Elijah, who lived in Gilead just across the river from Jericho, might have been there because he recognized that God was at work in Hiel's tragedy. He would have seen it as a fulfillment of prophecy. The Talmud states that Ahab and Elijah argued over whether or not the death of Hiel's sons was a fulfillment of prophecy.

Watch Jericho

When we left our drama, Elijah and God were talking about faith. Let's rejoin them.

ELIJAH: But my faith is so small, Lord; I don't know how You can use me at all.

GOD: It may be small now, but I can help it grow.

ELIJAH: How, Lord?

GOD: By demonstrating to you that I am alive and well and still able to fulfill My promises.

ELIJAH: I haven't seen many fulfilled promises lately. In fact, most folks around here think that You're not interested in us any more; some folks think that You are dead.

GOD: Watch Jericho, Elijah, watch Jericho.

Whether Ahab and Elijah met in Jericho or not is not known for certain. But you can be sure that Elijah was watching Jericho. And what God did in Jericho in fulfillment of Joshua's prophecy was a shot in the arm to Elijah's faith.

Why? Because Elijah remembered another prophecy made by Moses. "Beware, lest your hearts be deceived and you turn away and serve other gods, and worship them. Or the anger of the Lord will be kindled against you, and He will shut up the heavens so that there will be no rain" (Deut. 11:16-17).

The Talmud records that Elijah told Ahab in Jericho: "If the curse of the disciple (Joshua) proved effective, how much more effective will be the curse of the master (Moses)."

So when Elijah told King Ahab that he was in for an extended dry spell (17:1), he wasn't exercising faith on his own whim. He was believing a statement that God had made through His servant Moses. Elijah was encouraged in his faith by what God had already done in fulfilling the curse on Jericho.

I can identify with Elijah in this. My faith is very weak and fragile, and God knows that sometimes my faith needs priming, like an old farm pump. Even then I could never command the heavens to stop raining; but if God had promised that He would shut up the heavens, maybe I would have enough faith to trust His Word.

That's how much faith Elijah seemed to have at this point—just enough to get the job done.

Three Things for Sure

According to 1 Kings 17:1, there were three things that Elijah knew. And they were enough.

1. God is alive. Obviously, Elijah was on speaking terms with God. Besides that, the episode at Jericho must have been proof to Elijah that God was at work. The assurance that God was alive gave Elijah boldness.

The other two men in the story, Hiel and Ahab, had a "God is dead" philosophy. Interestingly enough, Hiel's name literally means, "God lives." But if he really believed his name, he would never have undertaken the rebuilding of Jericho. If he recalled Joshua's prophecy at all, he must have thought either that God was dead or else that God had a lapse of memory regarding Jericho.

Ahab didn't really believe that God was alive either. Otherwise, he wouldn't have felt it necessary to marry Jezebel. His marriage to Jezebel was a chess move. He, along with his father, Omri, believed that an alliance with the Sidonians was the only way that the nation of Israel could strengthen itself to prevent a military siege by its enemies to the northeast. So the marriage made strategic sense, even if it meant the introduction of Baal worship in Israel.

If, on the other hand, Ahab had believed that God was alive, he might have remembered the Ten Commandments, especially the commandments regarding the worship of other gods. And if he had believed that God was alive, he might have remembered that it was God who saved the Israelites from the Egyptians in the time of Moses, and from the Canaanites in the time of Joshua, and from the Philistines in the time of David. Surely that same God could save the Israelites now from the Syrians and the Assyrians.

We are too often like Hiel. We act as if God were dead as we rush into schemes and plans without a thought about divine guidance. While we affirm that God lives, we act as if He had passed away.

Like Ahab we worry and fret over the Syrians and the Assyrians in our path and frantically take matters into our own hands "to help God out."

But Elijah, who had been biding his time backstage in Gilead, now came out from the wings with his first speech: "As the Lord lives, before whom I stand, there shall be no rain" (17:1). Elijah may not have understood international politics as Ahab did, nor the building trade as Hiel did. But he knew something far more valuable: "God lives."

2. God is King. Elijah had developed a personal relationship with God. When he said, "Before whom I stand," he was acknowledging his role as a servant of Jehovah. Ahab had servants who stood in his court before him. They had been chosen by the king and enjoyed a special relationship with him. Elijah felt the same way about the relationship he enjoyed with his King. Elijah made sure that Ahab understood where his personal allegiance was. He was Jehovah's servant, not Ahab's servant.

Although nothing is said explicitly of Elijah's earlier walk with the Lord, something is implied. Later in the life story of the prophet, Elijah is quoted as saying, "I have been very zealous for the Lord, the God of hosts" (19:10). For years, no doubt, he had been deeply disturbed by the trends he was seeing in the nation of Israel. Yet there seemed to be nothing he could do. How could a young man from the hill country of Gilead have any effect on the state of affairs of an entire nation?

But there was one thing he could do; he could pray. James 5:17 says, "He prayed earnestly." The implication is that he had been praying in Gilead for quite a while. But nothing seemed to be happening.

True, nothing was happening that the newscasters of the nation could report, but something was happening to Elijah. In the process of praying and waiting, he was developing a personal relationship with God.

Sometimes our unanswered prayers give us time to develop a relationship with God. If our prayers were always answered without delay, we would not spend much time in God's presence.

Too often we maintain only a credit-card relationship with God. We keep inserting our credit card, promising God that later we will spend time with Him, but we never do. We buy now and promise to pay later, but we have become poor credit risks. Our credit card account is long overdue.

God didn't allow Elijah the luxury of a credit card. Instead, Elijah was forced to establish his credit by developing a relationship with God during his times of earnest prayer.

3. *God's Word is true*. Like the stone that David selected from the brook to slay the giant, this was the

missile that Elijah had that God could use to slay the prophets of Baal. Elijah was no supersaint; he simply had something that God could use. That something was faith in God's Word.

At this point in Elijah's life, there is no indication that God had revealed Himself in any burning bushes or had spoken on any of Gilead's mountains. At this point, it doesn't seem as if Elijah had any more supernatural revelations than you or I have. All Elijah had was a knowledge of God's Word and a belief that God could be counted on to keep His Word.

"In order to be effectual," said the late British Bible expositor A. W. Pink in his book *The Life of Elijah* (Banner of Truth, n.d.), "prayer must be grounded in the Word of God, for 'without faith it is impossible to please Him' (Heb. 11:6), and 'faith cometh by hearing, and hearing by the Word of God' (Rom. 10:17). . . . True prayer is faith laying hold of the Word of God, pleading it before Him, and saying, 'Do as Thou hast said' (2 Sam. 7:25)."

The writer of the Epistle to the Hebrews put it this way: "He who comes to God must believe that He is, and that He is a rewarder of those who seek Him" (Heb. 11:6).

In other words: (1) believe that He is alive; (2) diligently seek a relationship with Him; and (3) count on Him to keep His Word and to reward you for seeking.

This verse is the springboard into a magnificent chapter on faith, chronicling the exploits of great Old Testament heroes. Noah, Abraham, Isaac, Jacob, Joseph, and Moses parade before us.

How did they develop the faith that Hebrews 11 extols? By starting at the same place that Elijah started, with the three steps of faith: (1) they believed that God was alive, even when circumstantial evidence couldn't prove it; (2) they established a personal relationship with God by diligently seeking Him; and (3) they believed that they could count on Him to keep His promises. Then they acted on the basis of those promises.

With those three points as your foundation, you can become "God's building" (1 Cor. 3:9).

Why Did God Do a Thing Like That?

3

1 Kings 17:2-7

The hero: Elijah—or is it Ahab?
The villain: Ahab—or is it Elijah?
The problem: Well, there seems to be a slight disagreement about that too.

The Problem. From Ahab's point of view, Elijah was the villain and the problem. "That upstart peasant from the hills had the gall to come into my royal presence and bring a curse upon my land. He said it was not going to rain until he gave the word, and it hasn't rained since I chased him out of here. That whippersnapper Elijah is the problem."

From Elijah's point of view, sin was the problem. "For more than 100 years God's chosen people Israel have turned their backs on Him. Jehovah promised that He would send a drought if they persisted in their sin. And now that's just what has happened to them."

The solution. There was disagreement on that too.

From Ahab's point of view, "Put Elijah on the 10-Most-Wanted list. Send the FBI after him. Find him, at all costs. And when you find him, bring him to me. He is the cause of all our troubles."

From Elijah's point of view, "Repent."

The moral. Sometimes we are unable to find solutions because we have incorrectly identified the problems.

Ahab's point of view was earthbound, mired in his emotions. Elijah, on the other hand, identified the problem in the light of God's Word and went on to the solution.

In 1 Kings 17:1 we read that Elijah brought the Word of God to Ahab. In verse 2, the Word of the Lord came to Elijah. Remember the order.

Sometimes we complain that God isn't speaking clearly to us. We have a difficult decision to make and we want to make sure that we go God's way in making it.

Or perhaps we don't experience the presence of God in our lives. He seems distant from us, and personal communication with Him is gone. We speak perfunctorily to Him, but He doesn't speak back to us.

At times, we need to do what Elijah did. We need to act on what we know. We need to obey what we do understand of God's will before He will reveal the next step.

The Bible doesn't say that Elijah was moved by a special revelation to speak to King Ahab. It seems more likely that Elijah was simply acting on God's revealed Word. Then, and only then, came more explicit guidance.

Trained Seals?

Christians often act like trained seals. Every time they perform well, they expect to be thrown a fish. I don't know what Elijah expected, but I don't think it was what he got.

Here was this rustic from Gilead, exercised over the apostasy of his nation. He had mustered up courage to tell the mighty King Ahab what God had promised would happen if the people continued to turn from Him.

Suddenly the spotlight was on Elijah. He said his lines: "As the Lord, the God of Israel lives, before whom I stand, surely there shall be neither dew nor rain these years, except upon my word" (17:1). Exit Elijah.

He had performed his part well. Shouldn't he have been rewarded? Well, Elijah wasn't a trained seal, and God didn't want him to evolve into one. What God wanted Elijah to be was a mighty prophet, a sensitive man of God. And mighty prophets are a bit harder to produce than trained seals. They do not come off the assembly line in mass production.

I must confess that whenever I perform well for the Lord I expect a reward. And I'm disappointed when I'm sent away with nothing. Elijah, I think I know how you felt.

God's Servants Suffer with the Unjust

Do you remember Samson's last hurrah? Ten thousand Philistines were packed into the Temple of Dagon. Outside, the blinded Samson stood chained between two massive pillars. And Samson, with his strength divinely restored, did his thing. With a mighty heave he brought down the temple, crushing the Philistine horde. And also crushing Samson.

It may not seem fair that God's servant suffers along with the unjust. But that's what happened to Jeremiah. When he prophesied doom, the storm clouds struck him with as much vehemence as they struck his erring people.

Elijah had taken a bold step of faith in reminding King Ahab of God's Word, and what thanks did he get? Was he allowed to escape the drought? Was he immune from physical suffering? Was he rewarded by getting a more prestigious and godly parish in neighboring Judah?

No. Not only was Elijah a victim of the drought with his countrymen, but he also became a hunted man. Somehow it doesn't seem fair, does it?

By the Brook

There's no record of Elijah ever complaining, but since he was human, a question must have gone through his mind while he hid alongside of the Brook Cherith: Wouldn't it have been easier if he had just let the drought come without telling the king that God was the Sender and Ahab the sendee?

To tell the truth, it might have been better for Elijah. At least, then, he would have been free to roam his native Gilead without fear of the king's troops. It certainly would have helped him avoid the emotional peaks and valleys that marked his life. But a soldier who is told to storm the enemy lines does not ask, "What's best for me?" Rather, he trusts his commanding officer and obeys him.

Baal, the Weather God

Baal was the god of weather. Virtually everyone in Palestine knew that. Archeologists have unearthed images of Baal holding lightning bolts in his right hand. When farmers wanted rain for the crops, they looked to Baal.

So when Elijah announced that Jehovah was withholding rain from the land of Israel, it was not only a devastating blow to the agricultural nation, but also a personal insult to the powers of Baal. It was a duel of deities—Jehovah versus Baal—in the minds of the citizenry, and when Jehovah stopped the rain, it looked as if He were playing the game in Baal's ballpark. If Baal was good for anything, it was for sending rain so the crops would grow.

In semiarid Palestine, rain was, and still is, a valuable commodity. Normally, you can count on rain from mid-November to mid-January. This is called the "time of the former rain." In late March, hopefully, the "latter rain" falls; and I say hopefully, because sometimes it skips a year or two, much to the dismay of the farmers.

Besides those two periods, the most you can count on is a heavy dew in the mountains. So when Elijah said, "Neither dew nor rain," he was calling for a long, hot dry spell with no relief in sight.

There is no doubt that the drought occurred. Even the secular Greek historian Menander, in his work *Acts of Ithobalus, King of Tyre*, referred to its devastating effect in Lebanon.

Can you imagine the chagrin and embarrassment of Ahab and Jezebel? How could they persuade everyone to worship Baal, the weather-god, if Jehovah was shutting up the heavens?

They had built a temple and an altar to Baal in Samaria. Certainly the farmers would come streaming from all over Israel to beg for rain this year, but if Baal failed to deliver, those fickle Israelites might turn back to Jehovah again.

Frustrated and angry, Jezebel and Ahab knew they couldn't get their hands on Jehovah, but they could get their hands on Jehovah's servant, Elijah. If they could find him, that is. Where could he have gone?

A Place To Hide

One of my earliest recollections is of playing hide-and-seek with all my cousins on my grandfather's farm. Since I was the youngest, I was usually the first to be caught. And I remember going to my older brother and begging, "Help me find a good hiding place."

In the game of hide-and-seek that Ahab was playing with Elijah, the stakes were much higher. But I can imagine Elijah asking God, with the same earnestness with which I approached my big brother, "Help me find a good hiding place."

Of course, what I meant was, "Find a hiding place for me, spread your jacket over me so they don't see me, and stay there with me." Something I learned about hiding places in those early days of life: they tend to be lonely and scary.

Elijah must have had the same emotions: loneliness and fear. And 150 years earlier, David, who had had plenty of experience looking for hiding places, knew those fears too. David had prayed, "Deliver me, O Lord, from my enemies; I take refuge in Thee" (Ps. 143:9). But David could also sing exultingly, "How great is Thy goodness, which Thou hast stored up for those who fear Thee . . . Thou dost hide them in the secret place of Thy presence from the conspiracies of man" (Ps. 31:19-20).

Maybe Elijah knew those psalms. When you are hidden in God's presence, He takes care of both loneliness and fear.

Why Cherith, Lord?

It seems strange. It's like being sent back to the minor leagues after hitting a home run with the bases loaded in the World Series.

Elijah had emerged from Gilead to confront Ahab. He had performed that assignment nobly. And now where did God dispatch him? To a brook called Cherith.

Scholars have argued about the location of Cherith, but most of them feel it was back in unglamorous Gilead.

God does things like that. He sends us back home to Cherith when we think we are ready for confrontations on Carmel. Life is humdrum beside the brook; it's lonely. Even God's sustaining miracles can become commonplace there. But you learn lessons at Cherith that you can learn nowhere else.

Moses spent 40 years in a desert. Jacob spent 14 frustrating years in Haran. Paul spent three years in Arabia. Even Joseph had to spend time in an Egyptian prison before God elevated him to be prime minister of the land.

Make no mistake about it—Cherith will never be confused with Disneyland. But if the Lord orders you to Cherith, be assured that He knows best; your task there is to develop spiritually.

The German biographer F. W. Krummacher described the scene this way: "Come, let us pay a visit to this man of God in his new dwelling place. Dead silence reigns, interrupted perhaps by the cry of the solitary bittern, while among the heath and juniper bushes broods the ostrich. All is wilderness and solitude. Not a human footprint is seen."

In time of drought, you would think that the Lord would put you alongside a river, not by a brook. But most of us cannot be trusted with rivers. For it is when we look at the frail mountain stream that we realize that our trust cannot be in the brook; it must be in the Lord. Alongside a river, we would soon forget about God's provision and take the rushing currents for granted. That's the way we are.

Why Cherith? Why the lonely place? Throughout Scripture we learn that God leads us to where He wants us to be and then cares for us. Even in the commonplace tedium of Cherith, we will see His daily miracles, if we look for them. That little brook with the feeble supply of water sustains us; and God's special kind of ravens bring what you need every morning and every evening.

God will take care of you
Through every day,
O'er all the way.

We sing that Gospel song with a carefree lilt. And we sometimes forget that God's care is not always luxury class. God certainly took care of Elijah. No doubt about that. But Brook Cherith was not exactly the Samaria Hilton.

I doubt that Elijah complained about the accommodations. But he may have had second thoughts about the waitresses. It was almost as if he were at the mercy of those big black "unclean" birds. It just didn't seem right.

If God hadn't spoken so explicitly and told him that the ravens would supply him with bread and meat every morning and every evening, perhaps Elijah would have balked at the idea. Admittedly, black ravens *are* unique servants.

But those big black ravens were God's servants too. And Elijah would just have to swallow his pride and allow himself to be served by whatever servants God sought to use.

God will take care of you too. But don't be fussy about the servants who are in the employ of the Lord.

Why Ravens, Lord?

Ravens and ravines go together. Each evening, large flocks of ravens would congregate in the rocky crags of isolated areas. Even if the ravens hadn't fed Elijah, they certainly wouldn't have been strangers to him at Cherith.

But ravens are scavengers, they are nasty predatory birds. According to the Law (Lev. 11), they were termed unclean, and Israelites were forbidden to eat them. Why would God use an unclean bird like the raven to feed His servant?

Noah knew about ravens. After the rain had stopped, Noah released a raven from the ark and it never came back (Gen. 8:6-7). It was a good sign. If there is any food anywhere, no matter how far away, a raven will find it. Noah's raven apparently was able to find food.

In the closing chapters of Job, God asked a series of questions about His creation. One of them was, "Who prepares for the raven its nourishment when its young cry to God, and wander about without food?" (Job 38:41)

The answer is found in another book of Scripture, "He [the Lord] gives to the beast its food, and to the young ravens which cry" (Ps. 147:9).

Jesus, when He wanted to impress His disciples with the way God provides, used ravens for His example. "Consider the ravens," He said, "for they neither sow nor reap; and they have no storeroom nor barn; and yet God feeds them" (Luke 12:24). If God even takes care of unclean ravens, don't you think He will take care of you?

God fed the ravens, and the ravens fed Elijah. God could have used angels. After Jesus had fasted for 40 days and then was tempted by Satan, angels came and ministered to Him (Matt. 4:11). God could have done the same for Elijah.

But there were two things God wanted to teach Elijah: (1) God provides, and (2) you are not to despise the servants that God uses to provide for you. It may be more blessed to give than to receive, but often it takes more grace to receive than to give, especially from ravens; noisy, unclean ravens.

Why a Drying Brook, Lord?

Usually, when they tell this story in Sunday School, they don't mention that Cherith dried up. But there it is in 1 Kings 17:7: "The brook dried up, because there was no rain in the land." How do you think Elijah felt about that?

Apparently, there was nothing miraculous about Brook Cherith. It was a mountain stream that was affected by the drought as all the other streams and rivers were.

> Be not dismayed, whate'er betide,
> God will take care of you.

But what about when the stream dries up? That's what you might call a "low blow," isn't it? How would you have reacted to your water supply drying up? For months you have been in hiding from King Ahab. You have been thankful for safety and protection. You've even come to appreciate those big black birds arriving every morning and evening. It wasn't easy making those adjustments even though you've always been an outdoor person. Recently you have been restricted, have had to stay near Cherith because it's not only your hiding place but also your supply of food and water. You've learned to live with ravens and ravines.

But for the last few weeks you've been noticing that the mountain brook has been getting shallower. And now it's hardly more than a trickle coming over the rocks. Why, Lord, why?

If Elijah was anything like you and me, he must have asked the question too. He may have felt imposed upon by God. "Lord, I obeyed You in fleeing to Cherith and hiding there. Lord, I even obeyed You by taking food from those nasty, black ravens. After all that I've done, Lord, why did You let Cherith dry up? After all I've done, Lord, are You going to let me starve in the wilderness? Maybe next month instead of feeding me, the ravens will be feeding on me." Why, Lord, why?

Not everyone reacts to drying brooks like that. Some people consider drying brooks as a personal punishment from the Lord. "Cherith is drying up because I forgot my mother's birthday last year." "I lied—or swore or got drunk or had sex—God is punishing me." But God doesn't deal in personal vendettas. He doesn't "even old scores."

Kinship in the Dry Spell

Why do brooks dry up then? Maybe because there is more that the Lord wants to teach us. We can't learn everything at Cherith.

In Elijah's case, one thing he had to learn was a kinship with people. Elijah was a loner. People brought problems and tensions; life was easier without them.

The nationwide drought taught Elijah to depend on

God for his daily bread and even to depend on ravens. But he hadn't yet learned something harder—to depend on people.

For hundreds of miles around, people were starving. Shouldn't a man of God share in their sufferings? Shouldn't he know what it felt like to hunger and thirst? What good is a prophet without kinship with his people? What good is a Christian without sympathy?

In the New Testament we read of a fever in Peter's family, bereavement in the home of Mary and Martha, a thorn in the flesh for Paul. Why, Lord, why?

If Christ Himself suffered, you can be sure that we will not escape. But what is the use of pain? Paul told the Corinthians that when trouble comes into our lives, as it will, God ministers His consolation to us so that we may give comfort to others who are suffering.

> Blessed be the God and Father of our Lord Jesus Christ, the Father of mercies and God of all comfort; who comforts us in all our affliction so that we may be able to comfort those who are in any affliction with the comfort with which we ourselves are comforted by God. For just as the sufferings of Christ are ours in abundance, so also our comfort is abundant through Christ (2 Cor. 1:3-5).

Changes in the Dry Spell

Another reason that brooks dry up is so that we might be more alert to God's voice and more eager to listen for new instructions. When the brook is babbling, we often forget to listen to God. When things go smoothly, we can slide into a rut. Even at Cherith, which was certainly not Paradise, Elijah could assume that life was to continue without change. But Cherith dried up, and he had to look to God for new instructions.

Change is difficult for us to accept, but when a Cherith in our life dries up, we are willing to consider the possibility of altering our direction. Many Christians can point to a seeming calamity that opened up God's window of blessing to them; they were willing to be led to a new area of service as a result of the trouble.

God in the Dry Spell

A third reason for drying brooks is to teach us more about God. The Lord cannot reveal everything about Himself at Cherith. Like the blind man trying to understand the elephant by grasping its trunk, there is much more of God for us to discover than we can possibly learn at Cherith, or in any one place.

At Cherith, Elijah learned that God is a great Provider and this is important to learn. One of the highlights of Abraham's life was when he took his only son, Isaac, up Mount Moriah and began to prepare a sacrifice to the Lord. As his hand was raised, an angel of the Lord stopped him from sacrificing his son; instead, God provided a substitutionary ram. Abraham called the place *Jehovah-Jireh* which means "The Lord will provide."

But there is more to learn of Jehovah than knowing Him as the great Provider. "This isn't all there is of Me," God was telling Elijah. "At the next stop you will learn something more." You might think of Elijah being involved in a progressive dinner. He had finished his first course at Cherith and now it was time to move on.

Sometimes we don't understand God's dealings. We don't know why we were sent to Cherith in the first place; we don't appreciate the fact that God uses dirty ravens to feed us; and we certainly don't understand why the brook has to dry up.

The fact that we don't understand is simply a sign that God's educational process isn't complete yet. He's still teaching us and we're still learning.

For Elijah, it was time to go to a new school, very far away. The curriculum for the next course couldn't be taught to a lone man in a desert. It needed other people.

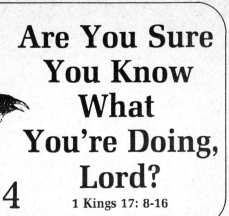

Are You Sure You Know What You're Doing, Lord?

4

1 Kings 17: 8-16

Quiet gentleman wishes to rent a single room near ample water supply. Kitchen privileges desired. Must have immediate occupancy. Write Box E, Brook Cherith, Gilead.

Well, maybe that isn't exactly how Elijah's ad in the Samaria Gazette read, but you get the idea.

What amazes me about Elijah was his patience. He must have been anxious about his lease expiring at Brook Cherith. He doesn't strike me as a naturally patient man, but there he sat beside the brook when it wasn't even a respectable puddle anymore.

"Are you just going to sit there, Elijah? Don't you know that God helps those who help themselves? Don't you think it's time to take matters into your own hands? The brook has already gone dry. What are you waiting for—a miracle?"

Perhaps Elijah remembered the example of his forefathers who journeyed in the wilderness only when the cloud moved. Whatever his reasons, Elijah had received instructions from the Lord to go to

45

Brook Cherith, and he was going to stay there until God told him otherwise.

Knowing the Lord's will is not always easy. Often we take the path of least resistance and let our circumstances decide what comes next. And so we vacillate like weather vanes, changing our courses with the wind. At other times we refuse to budge an inch, nearly demanding a voice from heaven to order us into action.

I once interviewed a medical missionary who had been used mightily by the Lord. His classic comment on guidance was "Even God can't steer a parked car." What he meant was that God expects us to be busy using our gifts and talents as best we know how for His glory wherever we are, and then He will guide us.

How Does God Guide?

Often God guides us through Scripture. This is not a magical approach to the Bible, opening it up at random and expecting answers to pop out as if we were consulting a Ouija board. But our ever-growing knowledge of Scripture enables us to avoid false steps and choose the right ones.

The Holy Spirit dwells within us and we need to be sensitive to His urging. He does not contradict the Word, because Scripture is inspired by Him. Usually the Holy Spirit speaks quietly to our hearts.

Often we are led by love. Since God is love, and we are to walk in love, such guidance is excellent motivation in Christian service.

God has given us brains to use. Occasionally we are led in ways that seem counter to good judgment, but usually God leads us as we commit each day to Him and then follow the good sense He gives us.

A fifth method of guidance is through godly counselors. These may be parents, church leaders, pastors, or other Christians to whom God has given a gift of discernment. The work of the Lord is to be done "decently and in order," and godly counselors can bring objectivity to a decision in which you are personally involved.

Finally, God works through circumstances. When a door is open, a decision has to be made whether or not to walk through it. It has to be remembered, however, that the devil can open doors too. So neither open doors nor closed doors are sufficient in themselves to provide guidance.

Elijah must have understood that. For instead of leaving Cherith when the water began to diminish, he waited and waited and waited. And finally, "The Word of the Lord came unto him, saying, 'Arise, go to Zarephath, which belongs to Sidon, and stay there.'" (17:8-9).

Good News—Bad News

To Elijah it sounded like one of those good news—bad news jokes.

"What's the good news, Lord?"

"The good news is that I want you to move. You've been at Cherith long enough."

"Good, I'm glad to hear that. What's the bad news?"

"I want you to go to Zarephath."

"Zarephath? Never heard of it."

"It's a suburb of Sidon."

"Oh."

I don't know how much Elijah knew of geography. It's possible that he had never heard of Zarephath before. It was a small town along the Mediterranean shore about 100 miles from Gilead. Zarephath was in the land of Phoenicia and hardly a household word in Israel.

Archeologists have dug up the town of Zarephath within the last few years, just south of the modern Lebanese town of Sarafand. In the New Testament it was called Sarepta (Luke 4:26, KJV).

Elijah might not have been aware of Zarephath, but you can be sure that when he heard the name Sidon, there was instant recognition. Sidon was Jezebel's home town, the capital of Phoenicia, and a city of commerce, immorality, and idolatry. Along with Baal, Ashtoreth was worshiped there, and since she was the goddess of fertility, the worship rites were lewd, to say the least.

Why in the world would God want to send him to Zarephath, a suburb of Sidon? It didn't make sense. If I were Elijah, I would have asked some questions.

"Lord, do You know what You're doing? Jezebel is after my scalp. Why are You sending me into the very shadow of her hometown?"

The Brook Cherith made a good initial hiding place. Elijah probably knew every inch of the area. He would have needed no urging to flee to Cherith. After all, Ahab would be after him, and if Elijah ever needed to elude Ahab's posse, he might be able to do it in the mountains and ravines of Gilead that he knew so well.

But Zarephath? He would be a stranger in town and everyone in a small town would know he was there. If he introduced himself he might be in danger of arrest. There could even be relatives of Jezebel living in Zarephath, for all he knew.

Well, God doesn't always explain what He's doing or why He's doing it. Sometimes he directs us into situations that don't seem to make sense at all. What he expects from us is obedience. Not a lot of static, or delaying tactics, but obedience.

The word Zarephath means "refining." Elijah may have felt that Cherith had already been a refining process for him, that he didn't need another crucible. But God knew better.

Moving Is Traumatic

Although Elijah didn't need to hire a van when it came time to move, you can be sure that it was still a traumatic experience. Moving is one thing that doesn't become more pleasant with practice. No matter how frequently it happens or how proficient you become at packing your china into cardboard boxes, moving doesn't become less irksome.

"God is constantly transplanting us," F. B. Meyer notes, and though you may grumble and complain about being uprooted, God knows that a transplanting is often needed to develop hidden aspects of your character.

I'm not only talking about moving from house to house. I'm talking about God shaking your complacency. Just when you think that everything in life is working smoothly, your Cherith dries up, and you have to make a major adjustment.

F. B. Meyer stated, "The quiet life is by no means the greatest life. Some characters can only reach the highest standard of spirituality by the disturbings or displacings in the order of God's providence" (*Elijah and the Secret of His Power*, Moody Press, 1976).

You certainly see this demonstrated in the life of Elijah. He never was able to settle down anywhere. Whenever he was about to get comfortable and call someplace home, the Lord evicted him.

Comfort Disturbed

There's an interesting verse in Jeremiah that relates to the danger of becoming too comfortable.

"Moab has been at ease since his youth; he has also been undisturbed on his lees, neither has he been emptied from vessel to vessel, nor has he gone into exile. Therefore he retains his flavor, and his aroma has not changed" (Jer. 48:11).

What is this all about? It refers to the process of making wine. As the grape juice was fermented, a thick sediment called *lees* settled at the bottom of the vessel. Because the sediment had a strong odor, the wine had to be drawn off into another vessel. Once again the lees settled, and the wine would be poured out. This process needed to be repeated over and over again to produce the best wine.

Jeremiah was saying that the nation of Moab had been undisturbed for too long and had settled on its lees. Because Moab had grown fat and comfortable, it was no longer an effective nation.

I suppose the moral is that you should be thankful when the Lord empties you from vessel to vessel, changes your circumstances, upsets your comfort. God is making you into a better vintage wine.

New Accommodations

"Before you go, Elijah, I want you to know one more thing."

"What's that, Lord?"

"I've arranged room and board for you."

"A wealthy merchant, I presume, on whom I wouldn't impose."

"No, not exactly, Elijah. The person I have in mind is a destitute widow who is practically starving. She will sustain you, Elijah."

If Zarephath's location didn't make sense, what can you say about its accommodations? First, Elijah had been sent to a brook, not a river; now he was sent to a poor widow, not a rich merchant.

It's evident that God's *modus operandi* may not be the same as ours. "'For My thoughts are not your thoughts, neither are your ways My ways,' declares the Lord. 'For as the heavens are higher than the earth, so are My ways higher than your ways, and My thoughts than your thoughts'" (Isa. 55:8-9). The things and places God uses may be less than what we have in mind but they are part of His total way. Paul explained to the Corinthians. "God has chosen the foolish things of the world to shame the wise, and God has chosen the weak things of the world to shame the things which are strong, and base things of the world and the despised, God has chosen, the things that are not, that He might nullify the things that are" (1 Cor. 1:27-28).

But why? Why does God choose to do things that way? Paul explained that too, "that no man should boast before God" (1 Cor. 1:29).

After sitting around beside Cherith for a year, Elijah was ready for action. It's no fun to sit on the bench and watch others play the game. Elijah felt like a bench warmer, and when word came to him from the Lord to change his mailing address, he must have thought that it was a call from the Coach to get into action. But it wasn't. The Lord was simply moving the bench.

We applaud service, but God honors obedience. We speak of full-time Christian service as the acme of spiritual achievement, but God honors full-time Christian obedience.

The question before Elijah was not whether he was

willing to do a miracle for the glory of God. The question was whether he would go to Zarephath, the headquarters of Baal worship, and be dependent upon a destitute widow. The question was not service, but obedience.

North to Phoenicia

Elijah obeyed. He began his cross-country trek through Israel to Zarephath, which was 100 miles as the raven flies.

He could have traveled north along the Jordan, and then followed the Kishon River Valley to the Mediterranean, passing Mount Carmel in the process. Then he would have had another 50 miles due north through the Phoenician coasts before he would enter the environs of Sidon.

But that would have taken him through the heartland of Israel, near the capital city of Samaria, where Ahab had his palace. And Ahab was on the lookout for Elijah. His picture would have been in every post office.

If I were in Elijah's sandals, I would have followed the Jordan Valley all the way to the northern boundary of Galilee, before cutting west to Sidon.

Whichever way Elijah made the long hike, he certainly had ample opportunity to see the effects of the drought upon his countrymen. No doubt he was disturbed to see the suffering and starvation in the land. No servant of the Lord should ever be immune to the anguish of people round about him.

But as he traveled, I wonder if he questioned why God had not selected this house or that house as a dwelling place for him, rather than the home of a destitute Gentile widow in Zarephath.

Jesus Himself mentioned this when He was talking

to those in the synagogue in Nazareth. " 'There were many widows in Israel in the days of Elijah, when the sky was shut up three years and six months, when a great famine came over all the land; and yet Elijah was sent to none of them, but only to Zarephath, in the land of Sidon, to a woman who was a widow' " (Luke 4:26).

When Jesus finished His short message to His friends and neighbors, there was an astonishing response. The Bible says, "And all in the synagogue were filled with rage as they heard these things; and they rose up and cast Him out of the city, and led Him to the brow of the hill on which their city had been built, in order to throw Him down the cliff" (Luke 4:28-29).

Why had a simple Bible story about Elijah provoked such animosity from Jesus' neighbors? What Jesus was really saying was that God's message of salvation was for Gentiles as well as for Jews, and that they must not restrict God's mercy and grace to one people. To the Jews, Christ's statement was heresy, and heresy deserved the punishment of stoning.

Do you remember how strongly Jonah felt about preaching to the Gentile city of Nineveh? Then how do you think Elijah must have felt? He was asked by God, not to preach at Zarephath, but to be dependent, totally dependent, upon a Gentile resident of that pagan town. And not merely a Gentile resident but a female at that. And not merely a female, but one who was a widow. And not merely a widow, but a destitute widow.

Perhaps God had humbled Elijah at Cherith, feeding him morning and evening by means of the unclean ravens. But there was more humbling in store for him at Zarephath.

Where Is the Widow?

How would you feel if you were Elijah, after a 100 mile hike, approaching the small town of Zarephath? God has told you to go there and stay. A widow who lives there will feed you. That's all you know. It's a strange town in a strange country. You don't even have a clue as to who the widow is.

You wish that God's instructions had been more explicit. You wish that He had told you how to identify the widow. You can't knock on every door and say, "I'm looking for a widow with food." If God had only said, "She's five-foot-two, with eyes of blue and wears a red carnation in her hair."

Sometimes God gives us detailed blueprints as He did to Noah in building an ark and to Moses in constructing the tabernacle in the wildnerness. Usually, however, God gives us only a skeletal outline and expects us to put meat on the bones.

Elijah may have recalled the story of Abraham's trusted servant who was sent on a mission in a strange land to find a bride for Isaac. He met Rebekah just outside the city and tested her willingness to draw water for him. (See Gen. 24.)

After a 100-mile hike, Elijah approached the gates of the city of Zarephath. Soon he saw a human form, apparently at work. As he came closer, he could see it was a woman, bending over to gather sticks.

He tested the woman first by asking her to get him a drink of water. After all, that is how Abraham's servant had tested Rebekah. Abraham's servant had given a second test—that the woman volunteer to draw water for his camels as well. But Elijah didn't have any thirsty camels. What he did have was a hungry stomach.

So as the widow was going to get water, Elijah

stopped her by making his second request, "a piece of bread." To ask her for food took faith and boldness on Elijah's part. He could see she was destitute. How could he impose on such a woman? How could he become dependent upon a person who couldn't even find enough food for herself? At least the ravens at Cherith were not being deprived of their food when they fed Elijah.

God at Work

What can we learn from Elijah's story? There are four lessons.

1. When God works, as A. W. Pink noted, He always works at both ends of the line. God led Philip away from a spiritual revival in Samaria, but God had already prepared the heart of an Ethiopian eunuch in the desert for his coming. The centurion Cornelius was looking for spiritual help and on the other end of the line God was preparing Peter for Cornelius' call.

We could say that the widow just "happened" to be outside the city gates picking up sticks at the propitious moment. But it wasn't happenstance at all. It was God, at work in both places at once.

2. It seems strange that God, the Creator of all, who owns the cattle on a thousand hills, who does "exceeding abundantly beyond all that we ask or think" (Eph. 3:20), should send Elijah to a destitute widow in heathen Zarephath.

Elijah, the servant of the Most High God, was begging bread from a poverty-stricken widow. Isn't it out of character for God to work that way? Shouldn't He have directed Elijah to a monarch or a property owner with vast resources?

Not necessarily. For God's blessings fall out upon the donor as well as on the donee. Elijah was not the only one whom God was blessing in Zarephath; God was working with the unnamed widow as well.

Two spies had entered Jericho and found lodging with Rahab the harlot. She assisted them on their way, but Rahab too found blessing from the Lord as a result.

It is no sin to be poor. Into the widow's poverty came great blessing.

3. God's work prospers not by the quantity of our giving but by its quality. There were many in the area who could have given Elijah much more to eat and provided him with more lavish accommodations, but no one could have surpassed the quality of this woman's giving. Like the widow in the New Testament who gave her mite, this woman gave her all.

Much Christian work is carried on because of the sacrificial giving of widows like the one in Zarephath. I've heard Christian leaders say that they are sometimes tempted to return gifts that are received from these who can hardly afford to give. But this would deprive the donor of spiritual blessing. "Remember the words of the Lord Jesus Christ, that He Himself said, 'It is more blessed to give than to receive'" (Acts 20:35).

4. It is worse to be deprived of God's Word than it is to be deprived of food. Jesus said, "'Man shall not live on bread alone, but on every word that proceeds out of the mouth of God'" (Matt. 4:4). However, it has been a tendency in every age to equate prosperity with the quantity of food that is available.

It was traditionally considered an honor in Israel to have a prophet of Jehovah stay in your home. But no home in Israel was found worthy. Instead God sent Elijah to the home of a widow in Zarephath. And she, though deprived of food, had something that the richest man in Israel did not have—access to the Word of God.

When Elijah asked for the piece of bread, the woman explained how destitute she was. She had only enough for one more meal, and then she and her son would face slow starvation together.

Elijah responded by telling her to bake bread for him anyway. "Make enough for me first and then make some for you and your son. If you do this, your food supply will last until the famine ends." (See 1 Kings 17:13-14.)

Steps of Faith

Great faith on Elijah's part? Yes, but it was faith nurtured on experience, on personal communion, and on the Word of God itself. Trace the steps with me.

1. On the basis of God's Word, Elijah had predicted a famine. It came. Elijah's faith spurted upward.

2. God told him to go to the Brook Cherith and be fed by ravens. Elijah obeyed, and what God said would happen, happened. For a year, Elijah had two meals every day, catered by ravens.

3. At Cherith, Elijah had time to get to know God better. In fact, there was hardly anything else to do.

4. Now God had told him to go to Zarephath and stay with a widow who would feed him.

5. Elijah arrived in Zarephath and found the widow, but there was one hitch. She had no food to share with him.

6. Obviously, God was using the hitch to test Elijah's faith, just as Elijah had asked for water and bread to test the woman's faith. If God had been faithful in caring for Elijah, wasn't it logical that He would handle this problem as well?

Male Chauvinist?

As you first read this story, it seems as if Elijah is guilty of the grossest form of male chauvinism. How could he have the gall to take advantage of this poor widow? But when you examine Elijah's actions in the light of the rest of the Scripture, you see the continuous concern that the Bible has for widows. Along with orphans, they seemed to be objects of God's special care. (See Prov. 15:25; Ps. 68:5.) They usually wore a distinctive kind of clothing, which may have been one way that Elijah recognized the widow at Zarephath.

The Law provided for their care through a kinsman-redeemer, and the story of Ruth in the Old Testament is a good example of this. One of the signs of Israel falling away from God was its failure to take care of widows. (See Jer. 7:6; Isa. 1:17.)

In the New Testament, the first social problem that the early Christians settled dealt with the care of widows, and in one of Paul's final epistles (1 Tim.), he gave special instructions on how the church should care for widows.

Elijah was sent to the widow of Zarephath, not to degrade her but to honor her. It was a symbol of God coming to her house.

And that's the way God works. We may feel insignificant and that God could easily pass us by. The widow of Zarephath must have felt that God had overlooked her and her problem. There were thousands who were suffering in Palestine. Would God care for her?

"The bowl of flour was not exhausted nor did the jar of oil become empty, according to the Word of the Lord which He spoke through Elijah" (17:16).

Who Said All My Troubles Would Disappear?

5

1 Kings 17:17-24

"Come to Jesus and you'll live happily ever after."

"I had many difficult problems in my life before I became a Christian. But when I accepted Jesus, He solved them all."

"Life in Christ is a life of ever-increasing peace and contentment."

I'm sure you've heard such testimonies. They make God sound like a genie who emerges from a magic lamp to solve all your problems and to supply your every whim.

Elijah had found out that it doesn't work that way. Life was relatively tranquil in Gilead before he began serving the Lord. He never knew what serious problems were until he became God's servant.

From the outside, Elijah's situation didn't look bad at all—a private room overlooking the Mediterranean Sea, a food supply that was guaranteed to last throughout the famine, and safety from the posse Ahab had sent to capture him dead or alive.

Actually, the accommodations were not much better than at Cherith. The widow was poverty-stricken. Since it would have been improper for Elijah to live in the same house with the widow and her son, he was given an "upper chamber."

Don't get the wrong idea about that upper chamber. Most homes in the Middle East had flat roofs, and many of the homes had flimsy little lean-to shelters built on the roof, to house overnight guests.

Much of the daily work was done on the rooftop. Clothes were sometimes spread to dry there. Grain gleaned in the field was often stored there. Children even played there. The rooftop frequently became the all-purpose utility room of the home. It is unlikely that Elijah had much privacy.

The Widow

The Bible only records three statements made by the widow of Zarephath. Two of them were complaints, hardly a picture of a "merry widow." If the Bible's brief portrayal gives an indication of her total personality, she was a complainer.

Admittedly, her lot in life had been hard. She had lost her husband, and she had been left with a son to raise. No friends or relatives had come to her aid, and she was left to struggle through life as best she could. It would be natural to become a complainer in such circumstances and such people are just not easy to live around. Often complainers can make happy people feel frustrated.

If Elijah knew any of Solomon's proverbs, he probably thought of two of them as being very appropriate.

Better the corner of a loft to live in
Than a house shared with a scolding woman.

Better to live in a desert land
Than with a scolding and irritable woman.
(Prov. 21:9, 19, Jerusalem Bible)

Same Old Miracle

The widow of Zarephath, her son, and Elijah were living by the grace of God with a miracle every day as the "barrel of meal wasted not" and the cruse of oil did not fail. But human nature being as it is, even a daily miracle can become commonplace when it's the same one every day. Suppose you had to eat exactly the same meal, day in and day out, for more than two years. Would you complain about the lack of variety on your menu?

The Israelites in the wilderness, fed miraculously with manna, were soon unhappy because they didn't have other things on their dinner plates.

"Manna, manna, all we see is manna. Back in Egypt we had fish, cucumbers, melons, leeks, onions and garlic. Those were the days." (See Num. 11:4-6.)

It's easy for us to complain, too. We overlook the spiritual miracles that He provides everyday and covet after something that we don't have. There will always be somebody with more than we have.

I suppose that Elijah could have complained about how wicked King Ahab was living in a fabulous ivory palace, while God's servant Elijah was on the rooftop of a widow's hovel in Zarephath. It hardly seems right.

Job's wife advised her husband, "Curse God and die." She was facing up to the inequities of life and, like the widow of Zarephath, she didn't like what she saw.

Job couldn't make any sense out of the puzzle

either. But he could still affirm, "I know that my Redeemer lives" (Job 19:25).

Maybe that was part of the problem for the widow of Zarephath. The personal pronoun *my* was missing from her talk about God. When she first addressed Elijah, she said, "As the Lord thy God liveth." She knew that Elijah was on speaking terms with God, but it was a relationship that she apparently didn't share.

Cures for Complaining

Two concepts should help us to rise above complaining: (1) the knowledge that God is great, and (2) the knowledge that God is good.

The miraculous provision at Zarephath should have been abundant proof that God was both great and good. But a chronic complainer can always find sources of discontent. And it is a fact that problems don't go away. There are things we can't figure out. God's schedule is not always in accordance with our timetable.

So let's add a third point to our complaint remedy: (3) talk to God directly about the things you can't figure out.

The great men of God in the Old Testament were not those who could always add up the totals in the same way that God did. But they were men who were willing to go directly to God about the discrepancies and work out the problems with Him.

A Widow Alone

Suddenly something happened that took both the widow and the prophet by surprise. Her son "became sick, and his sickness was so severe, that there was no breath left in him" (17:17).

The widow was thrown into despair. For her it

meant a life doomed to loneliness. No relatives cared for her, and there is no indication of friends. Her entire life was wrapped up in her son, and now God had taken his life.

It also meant hopelessness for her. As long as she had a son, she could anticipate someone to take care of her in her old age. She looked forward to the day when she wouldn't have to scrape and beg for the next meal. When her son grew up and got a job, he could look after her and provide for her. But now he was gone.

It also meant meaninglessness. What was the purpose of life anyway? Her life had been filled with disaster and disappointment. The only bright spot in her otherwise drab life was that she had brought a son into the world. She looked forward to the time when her child would grow up, marry, have children of his own, and so perpetuate the family name. This would give purpose and meaning to her life.

The heavy burdens of loneliness, hopelessness, and meaninglessness wracked her soul. She lashed out at Elijah, sorrow and anger cascading out of her anguished soul.

"It's all your fault, Elijah. This would never have happened if you hadn't shown up." (See 17:18.)

Never mind that Elijah's faith had preserved her life for months; never mind that the meal and oil had been miraculously replenished day after day.

At times of crisis, logic can give way to despair. You would think that she would turn to the prophet and say, "Do something quickly, Elijah. Perform another miracle." Instead of turning to him for another miracle, she turned away from him and blamed him for her son's death.

It seems to be a human characteristic that when we

are involved in a tragedy, we want someone or something to blame. But something else was bothering the widow of Zarephath. "'You have come to me to bring my iniquity to remembrance.'" At first, she blamed Elijah, but her deeper feeling was hostility toward herself.

She may have done a lot of complaining in life. God was at fault, relatives were at fault, neighbors were at fault, but the truth that she never could admit to herself was that she was at fault. The ugly specter of past sin could not be made to disappear. Unresolved guilt feelings would not go away.

What was the sin that was plaguing her? Was it worship of Baal? Was it immorality? Was her son illegitimate? Or was the guilt that she was carrying as heavy baggage something related to her husband's death? If only she had done something else or been somewhere else, perhaps her husband wouldn't have died.

No one knows. Her sin could have been an enormous one or an imagined one. It does not matter. What does matter is that it had separated this woman not only from God, but also from the man of God.

The writer of Hebrews tells Christians to lay aside every weight and every besetting sin (Heb. 12:1). In the lives of many Christians is the heavy weight of guilt for sins of the past which they cannot lay aside. Though they are forgiven through the blood of Jesus Christ, they cannot forgive themselves, and so they plod angrily through life, lashing out at God, at family members, and fellow Christians. Guilt destroys relationships; it eats away at the insides of a person until he becomes hollow.

The widow's emotional explosion may have uncovered guilt feelings that she had hardly been willing to admit to herself. And that explosion may have been the first step back to wholeness.

What Are You Doing, God?

While the woman was immobilized in shock and anguish, Elijah, man of action that he was, moved quickly. He said to her, "Give me your son." He took the boy, climbed upstairs into the loft, where the air was fresh and the sun was bright, and laid the boy on his mat.

Then another miracle took place? No, not yet. You see, Elijah, a man "of like passions as we are," had some problems too. He couldn't figure out what God was doing.

The widow thought she knew why her son had been taken from her, but she was wrong. Elijah, however, didn't claim to know why. And you and I don't find out "why" about many things in life. But as we look at Elijah and the widow, we can see that it's better to know *God* than to know *why*. Elijah, over the previous years, had developed a good one-to-one relationship with God. Admittedly, the ways of God still puzzled him. That confusion came out in his prayer over the dead boy. "O Lord my God, hast Thou also brought calamity to the widow with whom I am staying, by causing her son to die?" (17:20) A more literal translation would be, "Lord, why are You breaking this widow in pieces? After all, she is caring for me."

The question of *Why?* plagues Christians and non-Christians alike. The disciples asked Jesus the question: "Who sinned, this man or his parents, that he should be born blind?" (John 9:2) Like the widow of Zarephath, they had the notion that suffering is always the direct result of sin.

Jesus' response surprised them. "'It was neither that this man sinned, nor his parents; but it was in order that the works of God might be displayed in him'" (9:3).

God allows suffering for many reasons. We are chastened, the writer of Hebrews tells us, because God loves us (Heb. 12:6). But that doesn't explain why. It merely comes back to the basic "God is great and God is good." As a loving and strong Father, He merits our trust, even when "His ways are past finding out" (Rom. 11:33).

Christians who expect a fairy-tale existence after salvation often have a difficult adjustment. Even Romans 8:28 ("God causes all things to work together for good") seems to wear a little thin after catastrophe piles on top of disaster and calamity.

Why, God, why?

The Bible indicates that the "fellowship of His sufferings" (Phil. 3:10) is an exclusive club for which there is no waiting list. Somehow these sufferings are used by God to make us conformable to the image of Jesus Christ who suffered for us.

While the Bible gives many possible reasons for suffering, the Christian must not become so obsessed with the Why that he neglects the Who. Sometimes God delays while we ask Why in order that we might get to know Who it is that orders our ways.

When we are obsessed with finding out why, we lose our sense of proportion. We become like Jonah who couldn't figure out what God was doing in saving the wicked city of Nineveh. As Jonah sulked, he forgot to focus on God's goodness and soon lost his sense of proportion. When a gourd that had given him some shade shriveled up, he asked God to take his life. The disappearance of a gourd became a calamity, while the salvation of thousands of Ninevites seemed of no importance.

Methods or God?

Of course, Elijah asked Why too. "Why are You breaking this widow in pieces, Lord?" prayed Elijah. And that, in itself, is a fascinating insight into Elijah. You don't think of Elijah as having been people-centered. He sometimes seemed remote; his life-style made him appear to be a loner.

But here he was, pleading to God on behalf of a Gentile widow. Through the weeks and months that he had shared her home he had gotten to know her well. No doubt he had heard her life story several times. Together they had shared a divine miracle.

And yet somehow Elijah had not penetrated her basic outlook on life. Her outburst against Elijah and her cry against God indicated that the presence of a prophet in her home had not changed her perspective. She was still confused.

The prophet Elijah revealed a deep concern for her. His efforts to explain to her who God really is and what He expects had apparently been unsuccessful. It is discouraging when your witness appears fruitless in your own household. Some people witness to loved ones for years without apparent success. What a sense of spiritual frustration and spiritual failure this evokes!

And now, Elijah must have thought, God is ruining all chances of reaching her. What hope is there? But God had a better idea.

Elijah stretched himself upon the child's body three times, and as he did so, he cried unto the Lord. "Let this child's life return to him" (17:21).

It was surprising for anyone who called himself a man of God to have contact with a corpse. According to the Law, such contact defiled a man (Lev. 21). But Elijah's compassion for the woman overruled any natural hesitance he might have had about becoming defiled. After all, God had already used "unclean" ravens to feed him and an "unclean" Gentile woman to house him. Why should Elijah fear defilement from touching a dead body?

Elijah's humility and earnestness is shown in the fact that he stretched himself on the body three times. In the last few decades, Elijah's method of artificial respiration has gained recognition by medical authorities. It is now, after 2,800 years, an accepted medical procedure. But Elijah wasn't thinking of first aid; to him it was a last resort. His mind wasn't on the method; it was on his Lord. It wasn't the method that God responded to, but Elijah's prayer. The child's breath returned; life was restored.

We often get confused as we copy methods and forget devotion to God. We read books and magazines to discover new techniques, as if gimmicks could replace prayer. God, not gimmickry, was Elijah's hope.

A Boy Alive

Can you imagine the next scene? Elijah took the child in his arms and descended from his loft to the house where the mother was still wailing in anguish. Perhaps her head was buried in her hands and she didn't even notice that Elijah had come in.

Can you imagine Elijah placing the lad in the mother's arms again? Her tears would still be rolling down her cheeks, but now they were tears of joy.

In the New Testament, when Lazarus died, Jesus was at a distance, and when He arrived in Bethany, Mary and Martha let Him know that if He had gotten there sooner, Lazarus might not have died. Things are sometimes said in grief that would not have been said normally. But Jesus transformed that gloomy town of Bethany in the same way that Elijah transformed the widow's house at Zarephath. The dead one was raised.

In Bethany, Jesus said, "I am the Resurrection and the Life; he that believeth in Me, though he were dead, yet shall he live."

In Zarephath, Elijah told the widow, "See, your son is alive" (17:23). The 17th chapter of 1 Kings began with Elijah bursting out of nowhere to tell King Ahab, "The Lord God of Israel lives." The chapter ends with him telling a poverty-stricken Gentile widow, "Your son is alive." And the widow responded by saying, "Now I know that you are a man of God, and that the word of the Lord in your mouth is true" (17:24). When Elijah had first entered Zarephath, the widow had identified him as a man of God. She no doubt recognized him from his clothing as a man of God. But now she knew it from experience.

Many people today would not deny the deity of Jesus Christ. They affirm that He is the Son of God. They repeat the Apostle's Creed in church week after week. But they are like the widow before Elijah restored her son. It was only after she held her son once again in her arms that she could say, "Now I have experienced what I previously affirmed. I know you are a man of God."

But more than that, she declared, "The word of the Lord in your mouth is truth."

What word of the Lord had Elijah declared to her? All that is mentioned explicitly in Scripture is what he promised when he first met her—that her food supply would continue miraculously as long as the drought lasted. And she had been living in the realization of the daily miracle ever since.

But there must have been some other "word of the Lord." Probably it was Elijah's daily witness to her. No doubt Elijah had told her of all that Jehovah had done for the Children of Israel, going back to the time when Abraham was promised a son by God. He probably told her of how Abraham had almost sacrificed Isaac on Mt. Moriah, and of Moses and the struggles with Pharaoh. He must have told her of the miraculous crossing of the Red Sea and the wanderings in the wilderness, and of how Joshua led the Children of Israel into Canaan, and how the walls of Jericho had miraculously fallen.

Miracle after miracle. Could she believe it? Was this God greater than Baal? If all those miracles were true—the parting of the Red Sea, the manna in the desert, the fall of Jericho and more—then Jehovah must be the God above all gods. And Elijah himself told of being fed by ravens. Could she believe it all? There was a daily miracle taking place in her house, and yet she still had her doubts.

But when Elijah brought her son back to life, she had to acknowledge that Elijah's God was not only the Source of Life, but also the Source of Truth. So her statement was not simply that she now believed that what Elijah had been telling her was true, but rather that what he had been telling her was Absolute Truth.

Miracles

Sometimes we think that miracles were commonplace throughout the biblical record. But this isn't so. Miracles in the Bible are clustered during three major periods. The first period is the time of the Exodus. For about 50 years (1450-1400 B.C., if the early date of

Exodus is correct) a variety of amazing miracles took place. Then for 530 years, God seldom worked by miracles.

When Elijah came on the scene in about 870 B.C., people regarded the age of miracles as ancient history. We think of Christopher Columbus and Martin Luther as having lived a long time ago, but they lived within the last 500 years. When Elijah spoke of the miracles of Moses and Joshua, he was talking about something that had happened more than five centuries earlier.

During the 900 years after Elijah and Elisha, there were a few isolated miracles in the lives of Jonah and Daniel, for instance, but for the most part, God chose to accomplish His purposes through natural means.

Then Jesus Christ came and initiated the third major period. What is revealed in the Gospels is the greatest display of miracles this world has ever seen. Over 40 specific miracles are mentioned, and John said that Jesus also performed many other signs or miracles (John 21:25).

Since miracles are clustered in these three ages, it is not surprising that the widow of Zarephath may have been incredulous when Elijah told her of the miracles of the Exodus. And it is not surprising when our neighbors can't comprehend the miraculous events of the life of Christ.

Elijah could have told the widow that if she turned to Jehovah, all her problems would disappear. But he didn't, because it simply isn't true. Elijah's witness to the widow seemed to go nowhere until he demonstrated that God is the Giver of life.

Our witness to our neighbors will not succeed by platitudes, clichés, and wall mottos. But it will have punch and power, if it is backed by a resurrected life.

Resurrected life? But that will take another miracle, won't it?

New birth is miraculous; changed lives are powerful signs that God is doing unbelievable things today.

Resurrected life?

Yes, resurrected life.

Whose?

Yours.

We Can't Both Be Right, Can We?

6

1 Kings 18:1-16

One way and only one way! Right? Yes and No.

Sound heretical? How can you answer Yes and No to a question as basic to Christianity as that one?

After all, didn't Jesus say, "I am the Way"? He didn't say, "I am a way." Didn't Peter say, "There is salvation in no one else; for there is no other Name under heaven that has been given among men, by which we must be saved"? (Acts 4:12) Didn't Paul say, "If any man is preaching to you a gospel contrary to that which you received, let him be accursed"? (Gal. 1:9) and "There is one God and one Mediator also between God and men, the Man Christ Jesus, who gave Himself as a ransom for all"? (1 Tim. 2:5-6)

No doubt about it. There is only one Way to salvation. From beginning to end, the Bible is very clear about that. Elijah certainly was clear about it. The Israelites of his day thought they could worship both Baal and Jehovah at the same time. If one fire insurance policy is good, then two policies are twice as good. Jehovah may be good for tomorrow, but

Baal, the rain god, is good for today. That's what Elijah was fighting against. And Elijah was 100 percent correct in affirming that there is only one way to salvation.

But after salvation, God may lead His children in different, even diverse, ways. That's why I had to answer the question Yes and No. This was a lesson Elijah had to learn. And Paul. And John. God doesn't lead all His servants the same way.

Do you remember the problem that Paul had with Barnabas? Barnabas had been Paul's best friend for years; Barnabas had befriended Paul when everyone else was suspicious of him. Barnabas had enlisted Paul in Christian service in the church of Antioch. And the two of them became the church's first two official missionaries.

But after they completed their first missionary tour, there was a problem. Barnabas wanted to take young John Mark on the next missionary expedition. Paul felt John Mark was a quitter, since on the first journey he had turned back before they were even halfway.

Barnabas insisted; Paul said, "Never." And the Bible records that the contention was so sharp between them that they had to part company. Who was right and who was wrong?

Paul's next missionary journey was monumental. He went into the continent of Europe and began churches in many of the key cities of the world. God blessed his ministry greatly.

Meanwhile, Barnabas took young John Mark on another missionary journey. While the Bible doesn't recount the particular achievements of Barnabas' mission, it does mention that John Mark was developed into a productive Christian worker. In fact, the

Apostle Paul himself later asked specifically for him because "he is useful to me for service" (2 Tim. 4:11).

Who was right, Barnabas or Paul? Or was it simply the matter that God doesn't lead all His servants the same way?

John came to Jesus one day with a problem. He had seen someone casting out demons in the name of Jesus, but the problem was, he didn't recognize the man; he wasn't one of the disciples.

Jesus told John, "Do not hinder him, for there is no one who shall perform a miracle in My name, and be able soon afterward to speak evil of Me" (Mark 9:39).

In the early verses of 1 Kings 18, we see Elijah faced by a very different kind of guidance than he had experienced. Three years had gone by since Elijah the Tishbite had appeared to King Ahab (17:1). For part of those three years Elijah had been fed by the ravens beside the Brook Cherith, and for the rest of the time he was fed by a widow in the Gentile city of Zarephath.

Back at the Palace

Meanwhile, you can imagine what was going on back at the palace. At first, Ahab might not have taken Elijah too seriously. After all, what did that fellow from Gilead know about weather forecasting anyway?

As the drought continued, however, you can be sure that King Ahab and Queen Jezebel put out an "all-points bulletin" on Elijah. Elijah had said that no rain would come until he said so, and that was reason enough for the prophet to be the subject of a manhunt.

The Bible says that not only did they search every nook and cranny in the kingdom of Israel, but they also sought the assistance of all the neighboring lands

(18:10). So important was this search to Ahab that he insisted that the kings of the neighboring countries take an oath and swear that Elijah would not be found in their borders. How embarrassing it would have been for Jezebel to realize that her own father, King Ethbaal of Sidon, was unwittingly harboring the vagrant Elijah in the loft of a widow's humble home in Zarephath.

Of course, rumors were heard. Elijah was said to have been seen from one end of the kingdom to the other, but by the time Ahab had dispatched his troops to investigate, Elijah had disappeared.

This enraged Ahab to the point that he was threatening death to anyone who sent in a false rumor. Normally, a king of Israel wouldn't take away the civil rights of his citizens in such a way, but King Ahab felt that these were extraordinary times. In an emergency situation, anything was legal. Even killing the prophets of Jehovah was fair game for Ahab and Jezebel. After all, those prophets might be sympathizers of Elijah.

Meanwhile, the drought continued, week after week, month after month, and even year after year. F. B. Meyer paints the somber picture this way. "The music of the brooklets was still. No green pastures carpeted the hills and vales. There was neither blossom on the fig tree, nor fruit in the vines; and the labor of the olive failed. The ground was chapped and barren. The hinds calved in the field and deserted their young because there was no grass. The wild asses, with distended nostrils, climbed the hills to snuff up the last breath of air that might allay the fever of their thirst. And probably the roads were dotted by the stiffened corpses of the abject poor who had succumbed to the severity of their privations."

Gruesome? Yes. But whose fault was it? In Ahab's mind, it was totally the fault of that Gileadite, Elijah. If only he could find him!

Only one thing took Ahab's mind off his hunt for Elijah—survival. He didn't really care about the citizenry. He cared about himself, his wife, his palace, his animals, his soldiers, and his servants, and probably in that order.

His animals were his military equipment. If an enemy would attack him now, he would be hard put to wage a battle; without his horses and mules he would be at the mercy of a foreign invader.

The Word from the Lord

Finally Elijah received the word he had been waiting for. For three years he had been restless to get moving again. The word Elijah got from the Lord was simply this, "Go show yourself to Ahab, and I will send rain on the face of the earth" (18:1).

The previous chapter had opened with God's message, "Go hide yourself." Now came the message, "Go show yourself." "So Elijah went" (18:2). I'm not sure I would have followed those directions so readily. There would probably have been a dozen verses added between one and two to indicate my desire to change the Lord's mind.

"Lord, I liked 'go hide yourself' better than 'go show yourself.' Let me practice that one a little longer," or "Lord, why don't You just send the rain and forget about me making a personal appearance in front of King Ahab," or "Lord, I've just started a Bible class here in Zarephath, and it seems a shame to leave it right now."

I don't know how much Elijah knew about the manhunt, but he must have had more than an inkling that Ahab wouldn't provide him with a seven-course banquet when he arrived at the palace. Yet Elijah said good-bye to the widow and headed into Samaria where the famine was very severe.

Obadiah

We are now introduced to Obadiah. He was the man who seemed to be going the wrong way on a one-way street. At least, that's what Elijah must have thought. You see, Obadiah ran Ahab's palace. He was called the governor of the king's house, which means that he made sure that the royal family, as well as all the palace servants and animals, were properly fed, clothed, and housed. Sometimes the governor of the palace served as a chief of staff for the king.

And whom did Obadiah serve? Wicked King Ahab. Ahab, you remember, is said in the Bible to have done "more to provoke the Lord God of Israel than all the kings of Israel who were before him" (16:33). That's saying a lot.

Ahab had told his right-hand man Obadiah to go out into the country with him and look for water and grass to save their horses and mules. King Ahab would go looking in one direction and Governor Obadiah would go looking in another direction.

The Bible doesn't say how many horses and mules Ahab owned, but an Assyrian inscription, recently discovered, indicates that Ahab had at least 2,000 chariots. And he had to have horses or mules to pull the chariots.

Archeology also gives some insight into the lavish palace that Obadiah had the responsibility to maintain. Its walls were faced with ivory and the palace contained thousands of pieces "of the most exquisitely carved and inlaid panels, plaques, cabinets and couches" (*Halley's Bible Handbook*, Zondervan, 1976).

By the way, don't confuse this Obadiah with Obadiah the prophet or any of the other 12 Obadiahs in the Bible. It was a common name meaning "servant of Jehovah."

Well, you say, what's in a name? Maybe he wasn't really a servant of Jehovah after all.

Yet we read that Obadiah "feared the Lord greatly" (18:3). Some commentators have suggested that he may have feared the Lord greatly, but he must have feared Ahab even more. Others have suggested that "there was evidently a great lack of moral strength in his character," or that Obadiah is an example of a backslidden Christian.

The trouble with this interpretation is that the Bible does not condemn Obadiah at all. Yet how could he be the servant of the Lord and the servant of Ahab at the same time? Didn't Jesus say, "No man can serve two masters"? Elijah couldn't understand it either.

A Bed of Roses?

Obadiah spotted Elijah coming down the road and said, "Is this you, Elijah my master?" (18:7)

Elijah quickly retorted, "It is I. Go, say to your master, 'Behold, Elijah is here'" (18:8). In other words, How dare you call me your master when I know who you work for? I'm not your master; Ahab is.

While Elijah had spent a year in hiding beside a brook and two years as a recluse in Zarephath, Obadiah had been dwelling in the luxurious palace of the king. If Elijah questioned whether Obadiah was truly a servant of the Lord, I can understand why. I think I would have been considerably irked to have this finely-garbed servant of Ahab pretend to be "my servant." Yet there was another side to the story.

First of all, Elijah didn't have all the facts. He didn't know what Obadiah had been doing for the Lord. All he saw was Obadiah's clothing; all he knew was Obadiah's home address. What he didn't know was that Obadiah had been risking his neck to keep 100 prophets of Jehovah alive. When Jezebel began her prophet purge, Obadiah had rounded them up, hidden them in caves, and had brought bread and water to them regularly.

With the scarcity of both bread and water, it wouldn't have been easy for Obadiah to get enough to sustain 100 prophets without being noticed. But he did it, even though at any time he could have been discovered.

Elijah didn't know what it was like trying to live a godly life in Ahab's palace. He thought that God had given him the rough road; Obadiah seemed to have the bed of roses. But those first impressions can be deceiving. Nor did Elijah realize that God sometimes directs His followers in opposite ways to accomplish His purposes.

How could anyone serve Ahab and still be God's man? Well, how could anyone serve King Nebuchadnezzar and still be God's man? Daniel did. How could anyone serve Pharaoh and still be God's man? Joseph did. How could anyone serve Nero and still be God's man? There were Christians in Nero's household (Phil. 4:22), and Paul never told them to change jobs.

Inside the System

Often new Christians feel that God must want them to avoid all contact with the world. They can understand how God's will might lead them to the Brook

Cherith, but they could not fathom how it might lead them to manage the palace for King Ahab.

At times God tells His followers to "bloom where they are planted," even though the climate might not seem to be conducive to growth. Family situations may seem intolerable and yet God may ask you to stay to bear witness for Christ in the midst of the situation. Working conditions may seem unbearable and yet God may want you to stay right there.

As a rule, Christians do not help a situation by withdrawing from it. Jesus told some of those to whom He had ministered to go home and tell what God had done for them. Yet to others, He said that they should leave everything, withdraw from their livelihood and follow Him.

There is no clear-cut answer to what Christians should do as they seek to cope with the world. "In the world, but not of it," is how Jesus referred to His followers in His High Priestly prayer (John 17).

We are to be the salt of the earth and the light of the world, Jesus said, and that supports the idea that we should infiltrate the world for Christ. But He also used expressions like "shaking the dust off our feet" when our witness is refused. And that supports the idea of separating from the world system.

Can a Christian bear witness most effectively by ministering within the system as Obadiah sought to do, or by testifying from without, as Elijah did? God has used His servants in both ways.

Before the time of Elijah, God's prophets were usually residents of the King's court. The prophet Nathan was a good example of this. When David sinned with Bathsheba, it was the Prophet Nathan who went to David, told his dramatic story of the wealthy landowner who stole a sheep from his poverty-stricken neighbor, and closed his tale with the words "Thou art the man" (2 Sam. 12:1-7). Nathan and other prophets of that era were advisors to the king, ministering from within the system.

The problem was that sometimes the system corrupted the prophet, instead of the prophet purifying the system. Sometimes the prophet told the king merely what he wanted to hear, because, after all, it was the king who signed his paycheck.

Elijah was the first in a new breed of prophets. He spoke to the system from without. As far as he was concerned, there was no way that he could exist as a prophet within the palace of King Ahab. Of necessity, he had to leave. (The 100 prophets that Obadiah maintained knew that Elijah's course was the only course that a true prophet of God could follow.)

But Obadiah was a layman whom God had placed in a crucial position. A. W. Pink stated, "There is nothing wrong in a child of God holding a position of influence if he can do so without the sacrifice of principle. And indeed, it may enable him to render valuable service to the cause of God. . . . As the governor of Ahab's household, Obadiah was undoubtedly in a most difficult and dangerous position, yet so far from bowing his knee to Baal he was instrumental in saving the lives of many of God's servants. Though surrounded by so many temptations he preserved his integrity."

Caution VS Impulsiveness

There was yet another difference between the two men. Obadiah was a cautious man; Elijah was a bold, impulsive one. Obadiah was a prudent manager; Elijah was a courageous adventurer. Most of Obadiah's life was inside; most of Elijah's life was outdoors.

So when Elijah told Obadiah to give word to Ahab that he wanted to meet the king, Obadiah was cautious, perhaps even fearsome.

Smuggling food and water from under Ahab's nose to 100 prophets was not a project for a reckless entrepreneur. The only way he could have survived in Ahab's palace was by living cautiously.

Obadiah told Elijah that Ahab was known to chop a person's head off when a false rumor of Elijah's whereabouts was reported to him. Even though he was Ahab's governor, Obadiah's head was quite detachable.

It's interesting to see that while Elijah didn't know all there was to know about Obadiah, on the other hand, Obadiah didn't know all there was about Elijah. Apparently, rumors had been flying throughout Israel about Elijah. It was said that he could disappear in one part of the country and materialize in another part.

Speak about flying saucers; the Israelites looked upon Elijah as a flying prophet. And Obadiah, who had heard all the rumors about Elijah, half believed them. It seemed as if Elijah were playing games with Ahab (if the rumors were to be trusted) and Ahab was in no mood to play games.

Nor was Obadiah. So he brought Elijah up to date on what had been going on in Israel for the past three years, and Elijah then promised that he would not go into hiding again. He would meet Ahab face to face. In fact, he promised in the name of the Lord of Hosts.

A God of Resource and Holiness

Notice the difference between what Elijah said to King Ahab (17:1), and to Ahab's servant (18:15). To Ahab, he predicted drought, "as the Lord, the God of

Israel, lives." To Obadiah, he gave assurances that he would not disappear, "as the Lord of hosts lives."

The *Lord of hosts* or *Jehovah Sabaoth* was a name applied to God quite frequently by Isaiah and Jeremiah, but not at all in the first books of the Old Testament. It refers primarily to the heavenly hosts of angels who serve the Almighty and the children of the Almighty as well. When the holiness of God is stressed, the name *Jehovah Sabaoth* is often used. And when God's children need to be reminded of the armies of angelic hosts that God has on His side, you find that name frequently mentioned.

For instance, when David confronted Goliath, he said he came in the name of the Lord of hosts. Though the army of the Philistines was encamped on all sides, David knew that his God had a more powerful army.

And when Isaiah had his vision of "the Lord sitting upon a throne," he heard the seraphim cry, "Holy, holy, holy is the Lord of hosts" (Isa. 6:1, 3).

Two thoughts come through. One is that we have unlimited resources. God is guarding us and watching over us in ways we do not understand. Heavenly aid is available for those who put their trust in Jehovah Sabaoth. The other is that this is a holy God whom we worship. Even the angels are awe-stricken in His presence.

No doubt Elijah wanted to remind Obadiah of both these truths. What he was saying to Obadiah was this: The God of hosts is alive. Living in Ahab's palace, you must be very much aware of Ahab's might and power. But look up, Obadiah. There are angelic hosts all around; God's armies are far more powerful than the troops of Ahab.

And he was also saying that God is a holy God. Living in Ahab's palace, you must be tempted every day to compromise your godly living. Sometimes these temptations are extremely subtle, Obadiah, and so you keep before you the vision of the Lord of hosts. Not only is He mighty, but He is also holy.

For anyone whom God has called to live in the world as Obadiah was, Jehovah Sabaoth is a good name of God to remember. It will keep you from depression and discouragement; and it will keep you from letting down the bars of your Christian testimony.

Elijah and Ahab

The Bible tells the next scene very matter-of-factly: "So Obadiah went to meet Ahab, and told him; and Ahab went to meet Elijah" (18:16). But it was high drama, and all the characters in the play knew it. For cautious Obadiah, it would signal failure or victory.

And King Ahab? How do you think he took the news? At first, he probably couldn't believe it. No doubt he checked and double-checked Obadiah's story to make sure that it was really Elijah and not some imposter. All his pent-up emotion from three years of drought and famine must have surfaced. As he rode his chariot to his tryst with Elijah, he too was apprehensive. Was Elijah finally going to call off the drought? He wouldn't let Elijah out of his sight again. If Elijah proved difficult, he would have to be killed.

He looked upon Elijah as a magician, not as a messenger from God. He thought of the drought as an evil spell, not as a fulfilled prophecy that he had brought upon himself. In fact, he didn't feel guilty at all. He had been doing what was in the best interests of his country. It was Elijah who was the guilty party. He was the traitor to his land. He was the rebel.

What was wrong in bringing Baal worship into the

country? Certainly Jehovah shouldn't mind having a little help. After all, Baal was the rain god, wasn't he? Two gods are better than one. And Ahab, who named his children in honor of Jehovah and who built his wife a temple in honor of Baal, wanted to have it both ways.

Of course, Jezebel was a bit more fanatical as a Baal worshiper than he thought she would be. Her order to kill all the prophets of Jehovah went a little further than he would have directed, but you have to understand that Jezebel only wanted what was best for the country. Those prophets of doom stood in the way of progress, peace, and prosperity for Israel.

And Elijah himself? Well, how would you have felt if you were in Elijah's shoes? A bit scared? That would be understandable. Elijah was as human as you are. And any time you come face to face with a king, it's an awesome experience. Especially with a king like Ahab. And especially when the king has been hunting for you for three years.

I suppose Elijah was excited too. For three years he had been sitting around, doing very little, anxious for this day to come. But if Elijah was only scared and excited, the dramatic story in the next chapter would never have taken place.

Ebenezer

About 200 years earlier, the prophet-priest Samuel took a bunch of scared Israelites and, with the help of God, routed the invading Philistines. After the battle Samuel erected a marker at the spot, and called it *Ebenezer*, saying "Hitherto hath the Lord helped us" (1 Sam. 7:12). God who has helped us in the past will continue to help in the future.

I think Elijah may have been thinking *Ebenezer*, as

he waited for Ahab to come down the dusty dirt road in his royal chariot. God had helped in the past—in that first meeting with Ahab, by keeping His promise and sending the drought. God had helped at the Brook Cherith, by sending ravens to feed him and keeping Ahab's troops away from him. And at Zarephath, by directing him to the right woman, by multiplying the widow's oil each day, and then by raising the widow's son. And God would help tomorrow. It's easy to feel anxiety about tomorrow. Who knows what it will hold? Fear and anxiety may rob us of rest if we do not know the God of Ebenezer. "Hitherto hath the Lord helped us." The trusting Christian delights in counting the times hitherto, when the Lord helped.

The trusting Christian also knows Jehovah Sabaoth. And why should Elijah fear, or Obadiah, or you, when the Lord and His hosts of angels are encamped nearby?

You and Me Against the World

7

1 Kings 18:17-46

I don't know who invented mountaintop experiences. It might have been Moses at Mount Sinai; or Peter, James, and John on the Mount of Transfiguration. But my vote goes to Elijah on Mount Carmel. That was a real mountaintop experience.

For three years, tensions had accelerated. The showdown was at hand. The confrontation on Carmel reminds me of those western movies where the good guy and the bad guy meet on Main Street in Dusty Gulch. This is the climax. There is no retreat. It's win or lose.

The Mount Carmel summit conference between Elijah and the 450 prophets of Baal was set up by a mini-summit, involving Elijah and King Ahab.

According to the Greek Septuagint, Ahab came running to this meeting. And there was good reason for his excitement. When Obadiah had told him that Elijah wanted to see him, he was sure he knew why. Three years ago, Elijah had told him it wouldn't rain until he said so. Undoubtedly, this was the time that Elijah had chosen to give the word.

As eager as Ahab was to see Elijah, he wouldn't want his eagerness to be misunderstood as subservience. After all, he was still the king, while Elijah was one of his subjects, and a very troublesome one at that.

The two men came toward each other. Some paces behind the king stood his aides, his guards, his coachmen. Behind Elijah—a dusty road, a stray sheep, maybe. No visible support.

In the dust-filled sunlight, Ahab squinted and scrutinized the man he had not seen for three years. Elijah had changed. He was leaner. His face showed even more a set of strength. His eyes were like flint.

Kings have the first word with commoners, so for an opener, Ahab called to Elijah, "Is this you, you troubler of Israel?" (18:17)

It had to be Elijah, but no harm in making sure. His question was quite a contrast to Obadiah's, when he had first met the prophet the day before: "Is this you, Elijah my master?" (18:7) Obadiah recognized spiritual authority in Elijah. Ahab did not.

Elijah's reply left no doubt that this was the man he sought: "I have not troubled Israel, but you and your father's house have, because you have forsaken the commandments of the Lord, and you have followed the Baals" (18:18). It was a brash thing for a commoner to say to a king. And if Ahab hadn't wanted rain so desperately, Elijah might have suffered the same fate that John the Baptist did for pointing out King Herod's sinfulness.

No Backpedaling

Ahab was a calculating king. He seemed to have a reason for everything. No matter what he did, he always could justify his actions. He was never wrong, never to blame. Blame Jezebel, the citizenry, Elijah, Jehovah, but never Ahab. In the New Testament, Paul warned Timothy about those who were "seared in their own conscience as with a branding iron" (1 Tim. 4:2). Ahab was like that. As a result, no matter what heinous crime he committed, he could explain it away.

Some children grow up like little Ahabs, illogically explaining their behavior to excuse themselves. But children, like Ahab, need to be confronted with the fact that they are sinners. And that's precisely what Elijah did for Ahab.

If I were Elijah meeting King Ahab, I might have backpedaled a bit. I might have grinned sheepishly and said, "Yeah, well, this drought has been pretty rough on you, but you know how it is." Elijah never backpedaled. There was no reverse in his transmission.

In one sense, Elijah was a troubler of Israel, just as Jeremiah was and Amos was. When Jesus said, "I did not come to bring peace, but a sword" (Matt. 10:34), He meant that He too was a troubler, of those who would not obey Him.

Elijah could have told Ahab, "Let's call off our little feud. God was unhappy with your sin and now you've been punished. Let's let bygones be bygones." If Elijah had said that, he would have averted the confrontation on Mount Carmel. But he didn't say it because Ahab hadn't repented.

Elijah's Proposal

Instead, Elijah made a proposal. The Bible gives no clue as to when Elijah came up with the grand strategy. It was God Himself who gave him directions to Brook Cherith, and it was God who sent him back to Zarephath to find the widow, and it was God who sent him back to "show himself to Ahab." It is possible that the Lord outlined the plan for him in Zarephath, or on his way to Samaria. At any rate, it was a masterful strategy, as God's plans are.

Elijah was taking full advantage of the situation and apparently keeping everyone else in the dark as to what his real intentions were. He knew that Ahab wouldn't harm him until that first drop of water fell from the skies, so he determined to accomplish as much as possible for God in the meantime.

Elijah asked King Ahab to round up 450 prophets of Baal and 400 prophets of the Asherah to meet him on the top of Mount Carmel. The Asherah, sometimes translated "groves," was a wooden idol of a Phoenician goddess who was worshiped in lewd and immoral rituals. (See 1 Kings 16:33 and 2 Kings 13:6.) In addition, he asked Ahab to gather all the citizens of the nation to the site as well.

Ahab wasn't told of Elijah's "fire from heaven" contest. Ahab's mind was set on one thing: rain from heaven. He wasted no time in sending writs to all the 10 tribes under his control to make haste and come to Mount Carmel. Elijah would be there to make an announcement.

The news must have spread faster than Ahab's couriers could carry it. When you said *Elijah* and *Mount Carmel* in the same sentence, there was no doubt what it meant. Mount Carmel was always the first place in Palestine to get rain. Clouds would come from the west, pick up moisture from the Mediterranean, be forced higher by the elevation of Carmel, and drop the needed precipitation. People knew that rain was finally on the way.

Elijah was planning to rescind his anti-rain order.

From all over the kingdom, the excited citizenry trekked to Carmel.

I once stood alongside the Brook Kishon, looking up at the massive rock outcropping on the southeastern slope of the long ridge they call Mount Carmel. A mountain range of great beauty and consisting of many peaks intersected by hundreds of larger and smaller ravines, it extends about 13 miles in a northwesterly direction, and at its western end drops off sharply into the Mediterranean, near Haifa.

Mount Carmel itself is a promontory 556 feet high, 1,742 feet above sea level at its summit. Jeremiah referred to the mountain as "Carmel by the sea" probably to differentiate it from the city of Carmel, near Hebron. (See Jer. 46:18.)

The area is well watered, because of its exposure to the sea winds. Canaanites believed Mount Carmel to be the special dwelling place of the gods and so built sanctuaries to the weather deities on its heights. As the rain and storm god, Baal on Mount Carmel was given credit for all the precipitation that fell.

This was a fitting site for the contest between Elijah and the prophets of Baal. Elijah made it as difficult as possible for himself. He did God's battle on the turf of the enemy. I wonder if he thought of Obadiah, who had in a quiet way, been doing the same thing for years.

Baal's Side

In a surprising turn of events, Elijah, the hunted, the man on the "Wanted" posters, was on center stage. Ahab, the angry king, who had summoned the prophets of Baal, and convened his citizens in this covenant assembly, was now a spectator. After three years of drought, he was at Elijah's mercy.

Elijah climbed onto a mound where all could see him. The people had heard so much about him during the past three years, but few had ever seen him. This enigma of a man from Gilead, dressed in strange clothing, stood with arms outstretched to command their silence.

Then he shouted, "How long will you hesitate between two opinions? If the Lord is God, follow Him; but if Baal, follow him" (18:21).

Beck translates the question, "How long are you going to straddle the fence?" Another commentator suggests, "How long go ye hobbling between two forks in the road?"

Some commentators think that Elijah's phrase, "hesitate between two opinions" in the King James Version, should be translated as "hobble on two crutches;" others think it may have referred to the hopping kind of ritual dance used in Baal worship.

Elijah stopped, as if waiting for a response from the people, but no one uttered a sound. Then Elijah spoke again, "I alone am left a prophet of the Lord, but Baal's prophets are 450 men" (18:22).

What about the 100 prophets of Jehovah that Obadiah was saving? They might have been in the caves along the western escarpment of Mount Carmel, even as Elijah was speaking. Didn't they count? Well, as far as this contest was concerned, they didn't, because it was one against 450 on Mount Carmel.

Then Elijah set forth rules of the game. There would be two oxen, of which the prophets of Baal would have their choice for a sacrifice. Elijah would take the other. Then each side would prepare its sacrifice on an altar and pray for its god to send a fire to consume it.

Elijah concluded his rules by saying, "The God who answers by fire, He is God." And the people said, "That is a good idea" (18:24).

No doubt the prophets of Baal were pleased as well. It was their ball park. They had their choice of animals. And they outnumbered their opponent 450 to one.

Elijah, however, did rule out one trick they had up their sleeves. The prophets of Baal often built tunnels under their altars which would channel a gust of air to the altar. A slight flame could become a roaring inferno in seconds. The sacrifice would be consumed in a minute if there was a glowing ember in the right spot. But one of Elijah's rules was, "No fire underneath."

The prophets of Baal entered into the contest with enthusiasm. Much of their incantation was what we would call yoga. From early morning, they chanted their mantras and danced in ecstasy around the altar. But nothing happened.

On the side, Elijah ridiculed the proceedings. "Maybe he's sleeping. You might have to shout louder to wake him up." Baal was thought to be hibernating during the dry season, and rainmaking ceremonies were thought necessary to rouse him from his slumber.

"Maybe he's gone to the toilet," Elijah said next. The crowd in the plain must have howled in laughter.

"Maybe he's on a long trip and can't hear you." The Phoenicians were world-renowned sailors, and Baal was presumed to be watching over the mariners in their travel.

"Or maybe he's just thinking. He has more important things on his mind." In other words, maybe Baal didn't care about them.

The purpose of Elijah's sarcasm was not to enrage the priests, but to arouse the spectators. The priests, however, responded with even more feverish activity, "They cut themselves according to the custom with swords and lances until the blood gushed out on them. And it came about when midday was past, that they raved until the time of the offering of the evening sacrifice; but there was no voice, no one answered, and no one paid attention" (18:28-29).

The Other Side

Now it was Elijah's turn. Though the day was nearly spent, he didn't seem pressured. His calm behavior was in sharp contrast to the frenzy of the prophets of Baal. He appeared businesslike.

He called the people to come near to him as he repaired God's altar. Then he built a simple altar of 12 stones, one for each of the 12 tribes. He dug a trench around it, arranged the wood in place, cut the ox, and laid the pieces on the wood.

To make sure that no one could think he was using trickery, he asked for water to be drawn from a nearby spring and poured upon the sacrifice. Twelve waterpots were filled and then poured out until the water filled the trench (18:34-35).

When the time came to offer the evening sacrifice, Elijah approached the altar and prayed for God to show Himself as God; he asked that God would vindicate Elijah as His servant. His purpose in prayer was that the people might have their hearts turned back to the Lord.

And then the fire from heaven fell. It consumed not only the sacrifice, but the wood, the stones, the dust, and the water as well.

The display of power was awesome. The crowd

gasped, and fell down on the ground. Here one and there another, and soon the entire multitude began to shout: "The Lord, He is God; the Lord, He is God" (18:39).

The Rains Are Coming

Do you remember that the name of Elijah literally means "God is the Lord"? Elijah had begun his ministry with the words, "The Lord God of Israel lives." Now that had been proved to all the nation.

The fire had fallen from heaven. The great summit conference on Mount Carmel had ended in a dramatic victory for Jehovah and His prophet. Fire had fallen from heaven, but no rain. In Elijah's mind, however, there was no doubt that the rain was just on the other side of the mountain.

Through Moses, God had promised that He would close the heaven so that it would not rain (Deut. 11:16-17), if the people turned aside to serve other gods. It was probably on the basis of that prophecy that Elijah had begun his public ministry three years earlier.

But Moses had also said that if the people would serve the Lord, "I will give the rain for your land in its season" (Deut. 11:13).

As Elijah looked at the people with their faces bowed to the ground, he realized there was no longer anything holding back the rain.

One thing remained to be done—not a pleasant task, but necessary. Elijah told the people to seize the prophets of Baal—and probably those of Asherah too. He took them all down to the Brook Kishon at the foot of Mount Carmel, on the border between Phoenecia and Israel, and had them killed.

Then Elijah went back to Ahab and told him to go eat and drink, for the rains were coming. He said, "There is the sound of the roar of a heavy shower" (18:41). I wonder if anyone but Elijah heard the sound. Ahab had had the first word in their encounter. Elijah had the last word: Go celebrate. It's going to rain.

While Ahab went to eat, Elijah went to pray. And what a scene of prayer it was! He climbed toward the summit of Mount Carmel and bowed low in prayer. A servant was sent to look toward the sea for the rain cloud, but he could see none. When he reported back to Elijah, the prophet sent him to look again. Seven times the servant scaled the mountain to look for the cloud, and finally he was able to see a small cloud "about as small as a man's hand" (18:44).

It was enough for Elijah's faith. He told King Ahab to hitch up his chariot and head back to the palace before he got caught in a rainstorm. The Valley of Esdraelon, through which he had to pass, often turned into a quagmire during a heavy rain. (It happened in the time of the judges that a general got stuck in the mud there with his chariot and as a result lost a war. See Jud. 4—5.)

Before Ahab could get his chariot down the mountain, the sky had darkened and the wind had started blowing. But in front of him he could see the figure of Elijah in the dusk, running ahead of his chariot. It was about a 17-mile run for Elijah, who despite the rigors of the day, still had his adrenaline flowing. We read that "the hand of the Lord was on Elijah, and he girded up his loins and outran Ahab to Jezreel" (18:46).

What was Elijah doing running toward the palace? Did he think Ahab would hire him as the palace prophet to replace the 450 prophets of Baal? Did he think that he could convert Queen Jezebel? Did he feel that God would use him to be the instrument to bring a true spiritual revival? In the next chapter we'll try to answer some of those questions, but let's go back in the mountaintop experience for the moment.

Confidence and Prayer

As I look at Elijah in 1 Kings 18, two things impress me: a calm confidence based on the knowledge of God's omnipotence and sovereignty; and a high priority placed on prayer.

1. Confidence. Some writers depict Elijah as impulsive and reckless, but this chapter indicates the opposite. He faced an impossible situation with carefully-developed strategy and he followed the strategy through to its completion in a very business-like fashion. The prophets of Baal were frantic; Elijah appeared methodical.

Why? Because he had the confidence that God who had called him to do a job would guide, guard, and prosper him until that job was completed.

Why? Because he had compiled three years of experience of living day by day with God, in dependence for his daily needs. At Cherith and Zarephath, Elijah could never take a meal for granted; his food was provided by the grace of God. Those three years of dependent living had built up a faith that he could now use when the odds were stacked 450 to 1 against him.

Elijah had had a series of successes in his dealings with God that fed his faith. The manager of a baseball team or the coach of a football team looks at his exhibition season, prior to the beginning of the official schedule, as having three values: (1) to get the athletes in shape for the grueling season; (2) to enable the coaches to know the strengths and weaknesses of their athletes and (3) to establish a pattern of winning that will carry over into the regular series.

Elijah's exhibition season had prepared him well. He was not only in shape for the contest, but had also established a pattern of winning.

One of the biggest mistakes that we make as Christians is to disregard the value of the exhibition season. We tell God, "We'll take care of the small things, and when something gets out of hand, we'll come to You."

Instead, we are advised to commit all our ways to Him, and to thank God for the little victories that seem inconsequential. If we see God's hand in the small affairs of life, we can develop a confidence in His ability to work in the crisis times as well.

Maybe this is one of the reasons why such a common thing as grace before meals should not be treated lightly. If we truly acknowledge God as the Provider of our food, will we not be trained to trust Him to take care of us in life and death situations?

Our victories will not always be as dramatic as Elijah's were. But, dramatic or not, we need to take time at the close of each day to see what God has done and to thank Him for His work in our behalf.

2. Prayer. After the fire came down from heaven, Elijah told Ahab to eat and drink. But Elijah went to pray. Why did he pray? Did he think that God might forget the precipitation, now that the fire had been dispatched from heaven.

No. He was confident. But his job hadn't been completed yet, so he climbed the mountain to pray.

In the New Testament, the Epistle of James makes a point of using Elijah as an object lesson in prayer.

"He prayed earnestly for it not to rain, and it didn't rain . . . he prayed again for the rain to start, and it poured." That's a rough translation of James 5:17-18.

The way James tells it, it seems as if the rain depended on Elijah. Of course, it didn't. James knew it, Elijah knew it, and if you've ever prayed for rain, you know it too. When it comes to rain, God is the Boss.

But James always looked at the earthbound side of things. While Paul said that salvation is totally of God, James said, "But if I don't see any good works, I have my doubts whether God has done anything." (See James 2:18.) And when it came to prayer, Paul always emphasized what God was doing. James, on the other hand, was concerned about man's part. And for James, Elijah was Exhibit A.

Success in Prayer

In the Bible you can find many different styles of prayer. Nehemiah had the knack of working and praying at the same time. David's prayers were often long, and sometimes argumentative conversations with God. Once when Peter was having difficulty treading water, all he had time for was, "Lord, save me." If he had prayed longer, they would have had to give him artificial respiration.

But you have to be impressed with Elijah, at the climax of a great victory, while the people were still shouting, "Jehovah is God," while Ahab was getting a bite to eat, Elijah took a walk in the other direction in order to pray to Jehovah.

To the Christian, prayer is just as important as eating. It is a foolish man who would neglect food until his hunger pangs are so acute that he must eat to save his life. Eating is a necessary function of man;

and we eat to keep our bodies in a normal condition. Prayer to the Christian is that vital.

Like Elijah, the prophet Daniel knew the importance of prayer. Three times a day he prayed to God, with the same regularity that people took their meals.

In times of peril, everyone prays, even non-Christians. But the Daniels and Elijahs pray because they are building a relationship with God.

Most of us are geared to credit-card praying. Whenever we want something, we show our card and expect immediate credit. If we don't save for a rainy day, a credit card can always bail us out of a crisis. And that's the way some people pray. They use prayer as a plastic card to show to God, even though their accounts are long past due.

In his classic work *Holy Living*, Jeremy Taylor mentioned three things that he felt were the chief instruments in a godly life: (1) the care of our time; (2) the purity of our intention; and (3) the practice of the presence of God.

For Elijah, the practice of the presence of God had top priority. It was more important to Elijah to pray to God than it was to sup with the king.

But you say, if I had the success in prayer that Elijah had, I would give it a high priority too.

Well, if you can't identify with Elijah in his prayer life, maybe you can identify with David. Read the Psalms and see how David struggled with God in prayer. Psalm 22 is an example of this. Sometimes we think of this Psalm only as a Messianic psalm relating to Christ on the cross, but it was first the personal experience of David. He had three problems in the opening verses of that Psalm: (1) God didn't seem to be real to him; (2) his prayers weren't answered; and (3) even persistence in prayer didn't help. But David finally concluded that he had better not pit a few months or even a few years of frustration and failure in prayer against what God has been doing for thousands of years.

Earthly friendships carry the deepest meaning for us when we cultivate them over the years. But neglect cools any relationship. God becomes unreal to us when we forget the practice of prayer.

I titled this chapter "You and Me Against the World," because God and Elijah were working as a team against Baal. It was a relationship like that of a quarterback and his pass-catching end in football. The end runs down the sideline, cuts laterally behind his defensive opponent and then looks up, expecting that the pigskin has already been hurled and is descending to the spot where he will be five steps from now. Split-second timing is important in football and it comes only from training together over a long period of time.

When Elijah bowed in prayer on Mount Carmel, he was confident that God had already prepared a cloud, and so he sent his servant to spot it.

Yes, it was God and Elijah against the world. At least that's what Elijah thought. But while the headlines go to the quarterback who hurls the ball and the fleet end who receives it, there are nine other members on that football team.

Elijah had been running down the gridiron alone for so long that he forgot his teammates. But he who forgets his teammates soon finds himself sitting on the bench.

I Can't Even Touch Bottom Anymore

8

1 Kings 19:1-18

Several years ago on a hot summer day, our family attempted to drive from Mount Whitney, which is the highest point in the continental United States, to Death Valley, which is the lowest point. My wife and I thought it would be a travel experience our kids would long remember.

How right we were! As our car was trying to make the grade up the Funeral Mountains, just east of Death Valley, it gave out and we considered erecting a tombstone for our station wagon. It was unforgettable.

While descending into the foreboding valley, my wife was musing on the fact that God often puts the highest and the lowest close together. Mount Whitney and Death Valley, are only about 100 miles apart.

For Elijah too, the highest and the lowest were amazingly close. In fact, they were closer some days than others. Almost as quickly as you could say "Queen Jezebel," the mood of Elijah switched from upbeat to downcast. Once on top of the world with the crowd chanting "Jehovah is God" and King Ahab taking orders from him, he was now racing through his Death Valley until his engine collapsed.

You may have had trouble identifying with Elijah when he was calling down fire from heaven on top of Mount Carmel, but I daresay you won't have any trouble identifying with him in this chapter.

For some of us, the pendulum from up to down swings farther and faster than it does for others, but all of us face those long, grey nights of the soul from time to time.

Here was Elijah, a man of like passions *par excellence*. If he looked superhuman at Mount Carmel, it was another story at Mount Horeb (or Sinai).

But why? What caused Elijah to fall off the mountaintop into such a slough of despond? To find the answer, let's trace the biblical story.

Queen Jezebel

When we left Elijah he was leading the royal procession to the palace. He was exhausted, of course, but elation was written across his bearded face. Baal had been defeated; the rains had come; the drought was over; and King Ahab seemed deeply impressed by the events on Mount Carmel.

Elijah stood outside in the king's garden as Ahab went in to report to Queen Jezebel. The downpour of rain soaked his sweaty beard, as he pondered what might come next.

No doubt he wished for revival and for the reunification of the divided nation. He didn't know what God had in store for him, because his job description had stopped on top of Mount Carmel. Perhaps he hoped that King Ahab would lean on him for spiritual counsel even as King David had relied on the prophet Nathan, and King Saul, in his early years, had depended on the prophet Samuel.

While Elijah waited to be called into the palace, Ahab was inside, telling the dramatic story to Jezebel. In Ahab's version, the story revolved not around Elijah's God, but around Elijah. Earthbound man that he was, Ahab didn't see the events on Mount Carmel as Elijah had seen them. In fact, he didn't see Jehovah at all, because he had on spiritual blinders.

Elijah had predicted a drought on the basis of God's Word, but Ahab never thought of God's Word; he thought only of Elijah. During the years of famine, Ahab did not consider repentance or worshiping Jehovah; he thought only of finding food for his cattle and sending out search parties for the missing prophet.

And now as the rains pounded down on the palace roof, Ahab told his queen about Elijah and how he killed the prophets of Baal. The more he talked, the angrier she became. Elijah had hit her where it hurt. To Ahab, religion was all right if it didn't get in your way, but Jezebel was a religious fanatic, devoted to her faith. And her faith was the worship of Baal.

When Jezebel cooled down, she realized that the man standing out in the garden would have to be disposed of. The easiest thing would be to send out her guards to seize him and kill him. But then she remembered what Ahab said about the huge crowd that had witnessed the spectacular event at Mount Carmel. If she killed their hero, they could easily revolt. Half of Ahab's predecessors on the throne had died violent deaths and she didn't want Ahab to join them. Nor did she have any intention of precipitating a military coup to rise up against her.

But she had to get rid of Elijah. So she called a

messenger to take a message to Elijah. "By this time tomorrow, I will do to you what you have done to my prophets of Baal." It was a scare tactic to drive him out of the country again.

Elijah was stunned. Suddenly he felt very much alone. He had spent months alone by the Brook Cherith and two quiet years in the Gentile city of Zarephath, but he had never felt so alone as right now, standing in the king's garden with Jezebel's threat still echoing in his ears.

"By this time tomorrow . . ."

And as Elijah mulled upon Jezebel's words, he decided what to do. Run.

Not northwest to Zarephath. Not due east to Gilead. But south, straight south, through the kingdom of Judah, about 75 miles to Beersheba, the southern frontier city of Judah. But even that wouldn't be safe. He would have to go further.

Fear of Dying

Why did he run? We read, "He was afraid and rose and ran for his life" (19:3). The Bible speaks about the "peace of God which surpasses all comprehension" (Phil. 4:7). The prophet Isaiah wrote, "Thou wilt keep him in perfect peace whose mind is stayed on Thee" (26:3, KJV). Another version renders that verse, "The steadfast of mind Thou wilt keep in perfect peace, because he trusts in Thee."

The problem, of course, was that Elijah was looking at Jezebel and not to the Lord. He hadn't received any divine instructions for this occasion, so rather than stand in Jezebel's garden waiting for the ax to fall, he ran.

Peter, the disciple who started to walk on water, began to sink when he was afraid. Ten spies who examined the Promised Land came back with a negative report because they were afraid. The disciples in the storm-tossed boat feared in spite of the fact that the Creator was in the boat with them.

On top of Mount Carmel, Elijah knew that God was with him. Now he was afraid. Why was it that one woman could do what 450 priests of Baal couldn't do? She represented civil authority, and humanly speaking, Elijah had good reason to fear. His personal safety, even his survival, was at stake. Isn't self-preservation a good reason to seek refuge? As long as the drought continued, Elijah was safe, because Ahab thought that the mysterious prophet had a secret key that would unlock the heavens. Now the rains had come. As he stood soaking wet in the royal garden, Elijah felt as vulnerable as Clark Kent without his Superman outfit.

Most people fear failure. Only a few hours earlier, Elijah could almost taste victory. But Jezebel's edict triggered feelings of failure. Of course, 450 prophets of Baal had been slain; of course, the people had cried "Jehovah is God." But Jezebel could import 450 more prophets of Baal from her native Sidon and her purge against the followers of Jehovah would become even more vicious.

And the people, the fickle people, would soon forget all about the excitement at Mount Carmel. They would follow Jezebel's leading, and once again they would plunge headlong into the evils of Baal worship. Soon all of Elijah's miraculous power from God would be scarcely remembered.

Three years of waiting, a glorious day of triumph, and then the realization that he had really accomplished nothing. A failure. That's what he felt like. A total failure.

Fear of the Unknown

In addition to fearing premature death, and failure, Elijah was afraid of the unknown. Like the manager of a slumping baseball team on the last week of his three-year contract, Elijah realized that his contract had expired and he didn't know if it would be renewed. His commission from God was tied in with the three-year drought. Now that the drought was over, what was there left for him to do? He was an unemployed prophet. He could return home to Gilead, but that would be the first place Jezebel would look for him.

He wanted to serve God, but the job market for hunted prophets was tight indeed. How can you live free from fear, how can you have peace when you don't have a job and your life is threatened? How can you find tranquillity when you think that God has put you out to pasture?

There is an old hymn by Edward Bickersteth which asks that question.

Peace, perfect peace—my future all unknown?
Jesus we know, and He is on the throne.

In the courtyard of King Ahab, Elijah's vision was so clouded that the only person he could see was Queen Jezebel. The writer of Hebrews says that Moses, by faith, did not fear the wrath of the king because he saw "Him who is invisible." By faith it is possible to see the invisible, yet even Moses had his short-sighted moments. At this time Elijah saw only the visible and he was terrified.

The fears that Elijah faced are the same fears that confront you and me. We fear death and physical suffering. We fear failure and futility of life. We fear uselessness and an uncertain tomorrow.

When all these fears combined to descend upon

Elijah, the cloud was darker than the rain clouds overhead. And Elijah headed south, as fast as his legs could carry him. At Beersheba, Elijah left his servant behind; no one could keep pace with him.

Prayer under a Broom Bush

South of Beersheba was the wilderness of the Negev and then the Sinai desert. It was no-man's land. After traveling for a scorching day in the desert heat, Elijah collapsed under a broom bush. While the broom bush would never be mistaken for a mighty oak, when you are in the desert, any shade is welcome. Some translators call it a juniper, but it's really a desert shrub with long slender branches, small leaves, and showy yellow flowers. At best it grows to a height of 10 feet.

Elijah's prayer under the broom bush was one of utter dejection. "Lord, I've had enough. Take my life. I'm no better than my ancestors." (See 19:4.)

By the way, this is the fourth time that the Book of 1 Kings tells us that Elijah prayed. The first time, a son was restored to life; the second time, fire came down from heaven; the third time, rains descended after a three-year drought. But this time, God didn't grant Elijah's wish.

Elijah's prayer didn't make any sense. Elijah was running away from Jezebel in order to save his life, but now he was asking God to take his life. He was as mixed up as we often are in our prayers.

Fortunately, the Holy Spirit is the great unraveler of our mixed-up prayers. The lines of our requests sometimes come out as tangled as a skein of yarn after two frolicking kittens have played in it, but the Spirit painstakingly sorts it all out and presents it to the Father.

Reasons for Panic

Several identifiable factors contributed to Elijah's panic. The same things touch us, so let's look at them.

1. Fatigue. When you are down physically, you'll probably be down spiritually. It is not easy to be a spiritual giant when you are flat on your back. Sometimes the best advice that can be given to someone who is frustrated by spiritual failure is to tell him to get medical and/or psychological help or to stop for a good rest and needed nourishment. While it is possible to be strong spiritually and be exhausted emotionally and physically, it is not the usual.

Elijah was suffering from a severe letdown. Emotionally, he was depressed, physically, he was fatigued. His momentous Mount Carmel experience had drained him. It had been the climax to three years of waiting. Then came the grueling run to the king's palace and another long-distance run to Beersheba and beyond.

Jesus recognized the need for rest after a battle. In Mark 6, He sent His disciples out two by two into the villages, and they returned with exciting reports of what had been accomplished. And what did Jesus do? He said, "Come ye yourselves apart into a desert place and rest awhile." In the military, they call it "R and R." It's rest and recuperation after a battle.

Some of the disciples may have been perturbed at the idea of resting. Hadn't Jesus previously told them that the fields were white unto harvest? And hadn't they just experienced this for themselves? Why should the work be delayed?

But Jesus knew what His disciples didn't, and what Elijah didn't know. Spiritual depression can easily set in when the body is weak and the nerves are taut. The higher the wave, the deeper the trough.

In the life of any Christian, it's important to make provision for quiet recuperation after spiritual activity. This is one reason why ministers often take Monday as their day off. For them, Sunday is a time of intense activity, emotionally, spiritually, and physically. Often, they return to their homes on Sunday nights nearly as downhearted and discouraged as Elijah. But after a night's sleep and a day to recuperate, they are ready once again to face the spiritual challenge of another week.

2. False hopes. Elijah may have had the notion that the victory on Mount Carmel would solve everything. It would seem that Elijah believed that when the crowd chanted "The Lord, He is God" and when the priests of Baal were slain, the battle was over and revival had come. But Elijah had to learn that a victory in one battle is only a prelude to another battle.

Often, we face the same kind of disillusionment from false hopes. A woman prays for her unsaved husband for years. "If only he would come to know the Lord, our marriage would be wonderful," she dreams. But then he becomes a Christian in answer to her prayers, and a few months later she realizes that all her marital problems haven't been solved. And she becomes depressed.

Perhaps you feel that if only your church had a new pastor, all the church problems would be resolved. And then one day your pastor leaves your church and a new minister comes. However, the problems remain. And you become depressed. False hopes often lead to depression.

3. Disillusionment with God's people. Elijah felt let down by the people of God. "I, even I only, am left," he told God (19:10, KJV). He had heard the people cry, "The Lord, He is God," and for the moment he believed that they meant it. But as he reflected on it, he realized that they were fickle; they could not be trusted. And that is depressing.

I knew a young man who in his first job worked for a Christian employer. His employer seemed to have an outspoken Christian witness and also seemed to be a knowledgeable leader in his field. The young man admired him. But within a year, disillusionment set in. The young man found that this employer couldn't be trusted to keep his word. He was hypocritical in his Christian life. Eventually the young man quit the job in utter disillusionment; in fact, he almost quit the Christian life.

When your confidence is in people, you can easily become depressed, but when it's in the Lord, you can have utter confidence.

Yet Elijah's main social problem was not that he trusted people too much, but rather that he did not reach out enough to get to know other people. For instance, there is no indication that he ever got to know Obadiah, even though Obadiah was a man of apparent wisdom and uprightness. Elijah's despair was at least partly caused by the fact that he had no close friends with whom he could share his burdens and heartaches.

"Bear one another's burdens" (Gal. 6:2), Paul told the Galatians. But you can't expect someone else to bear your burdens unless you share them with him. Bearing and sharing go together.

You may be disillusioned with God's people to such an extent that you have retreated into a hermit's cave. You may say that you will never share anything of yourself again with anyone. But it's hard to be a New Testament Christian if you feel that way. Jesus said that people will know you are His disciples by the way you love one another.

Frankly, even though Elijah was declared a prophet of God, he didn't look like one when he was groveling under the broom bush. Although he had spent three years developing a vertical relationship with God, he had neglected a horizontal relationship with his fellowman. Christians who do not establish stable relationships in both directions are candidates for depression.

4. Shortsightedness. You don't usually accuse a prophet of being shortsighted. He customarily has a knack not only of seeing around corners, but also of seeing over mountaintops and into valleys. Some prophets accurately foretold events hundreds and thousands of years in the future.

Underneath the broom bush, Elijah had lost his bifocals. All he could see was the desert sand. If you are not wearing your spiritual bifocals, you too will frequently become depressed. Christians need to see long-range as well as short-range. They need to be able to see the hand of God at work in the full scope of history, but they also need to be involved in the close needlepoint of daily living.

It was the ability to live bifocally that merited inclusion into the list of heroes in Hebrews 11. In the Old Testament Joseph could say to his brothers, "You meant evil against me, but God meant it for good" (Gen. 50:20). And in the New Testament Paul could say, "And we know that God causes all things to work together for good" (Rom. 8:28). That's bifocal vision—a perspective we all need to develop more.

The Christian needs to have this confidence in God's sovereignty to carry him through the valleys of life. This is not fatalism or abandonment to cosmic forces, but rather an awareness that a loving heavenly Father is in control.

When you are in a valley, it is hard to really believe that a loving heavenly Father is in control. But He is. The omnipotent Creator is in charge of valleys as well as mountaintops. Even the valley of the shadow of death, David discovered, is merely a link between two green pastures. The Shepherd knows what He's doing when He leads through a valley.

Meet Physical Needs First

God first met Elijah's physical needs, allowing him to get a good sleep and providing him with food. Do you think it is unspiritual of God to tend to the physical before the spiritual? God knows what He is doing. In Elijah's case, no spiritual progress could be made until Elijah had food and rest.

For a New Testament example, consider the story of the Resurrected Lord as He made breakfast for His disciples who had caught nothing during a long night of fishing on the Sea of Galilee. Jesus had much to teach His disciples at that point, but He recognized that their physical needs had to be met first.

Some Christians have the notion that the physical needs of man are unimportant, but the Bible gives a proper place to them. There are times when, in order to meet man's deeper needs, his physical needs have priority. An angel provided bread and water to Elijah and then allowed him to sleep again. The second time Elijah was awakened, he was given more food and then the angel urged him to get going because he had a long trip ahead of him.

It's good to note God's mercy in His dealing with Elijah. As he fled in fear of Jezebel, the man of faith had become the man of fear. But look at the way God treated His erring child: (1) He gave him sleep; (2) He provided an angel to minister to him; (3) He supplied him food.

Sometimes we think God invariably punishes us whenever we stray from the course. But God is not anxious to punish; He is interested in restoring us. Sometimes it takes punishment to restore us, but at other times God uses merciful gentleness to restore us to Himself.

In God's mercy Elijah found his way through the wilderness to Mount Horeb, the Mountain of God, and specifically to a cave in that historic mountain. The cave is referred to in Exodus 33:18-23 in a very touching story of Moses. It was at a time when Moses had been experiencing an emotional trauma similar to that which Elijah was now undergoing. On the mountain Moses had received the tablets containing the Ten Commandments. But when he descended into the valley, he found the Children of Israel dancing naked around a golden calf.

From the sublime experience of the holiness of God, Moses had plunged into the middle of a heathen orgy. He was angry, and justifiably so. The tablets of stone he flung to the ground had shattered. The shock of what he saw had ravaged him emotionally.

At that point Moses needed a fresh start. Like Elijah he didn't know what to do or where to go. There is no word to express the emotional bewilderment that he felt. Why couldn't he understand what was happening to him?

What follows is one of the most sacred moments in Scripture. "Then the Lord said, 'Behold, there is a place by Me, and you shall stand there on the rock; and it will come about, while My glory is passing by, that I will put you in the cleft of the rock, and cover you with My hand until I have passed by" (Ex. 33:21-22).

From that experience Moses received a new vision and the Children of Israel were enabled to continue their trek to the Promised Land.

Fanny Crosby's Gospel song recalls that same cleft in the rock:

He hideth my soul in the cleft of the rock
That shadows a dry thirsty land;
He hideth my life in the depth of His love
And covers me there with His hand.

The Mountain of God

That was the kind of experience that Elijah, still confused and bewildered, craved. He knew he needed a fresh start, a new glimpse of God, an acknowledgment that God's presence and power were still with him. He found his way to the cave in Mount Horeb where Moses had had his person-to-person confrontation with God.

F. B. Meyer writes of Elijah's experience: "It is not difficult to believe that God loves us when, like Elijah at Cherith and on Carmel, we do His commandments, harkening unto the voice of His word; but it is not so easy when, like Elijah in the desert, we lie stranded. . . . Yet we must learn to know and believe the constancy of the love of God. We may not feel it. We may deem it shut up and gone forever. . . . But nevertheless, it has not altered. Staunch as the affection of a friend, true as the love of a mother, the love of God abides unchangeable as Himself."

In Mount Horeb's cave, God spoke to the depressed Elijah. Previously when God had spoken to Elijah, He had given him moving orders. "Go to

Cherith. . . . Go to Zarephath. . . . Go to King Ahab." But God had given Elijah no orders to go to Mount Horeb, and so He asked the question: "What are you doing here, Elijah?" (19:9)

It was a penetrating question, but not a scolding one, probably asked in the same way that Jesus asked questions of the depressed Emmaus disciples (Luke 24). Or of a depressed Simon Peter, "Lovest thou Me?" (John 21) It was asked, as a counselor probes, to find the root of a problem.

Elijah responded as a typical counselee, by telling his life story. Of course, God already knew what Elijah had done and why he had done it, but Elijah had no one to talk to, and now he found Jehovah to be a ready listener. Before long, all of Elijah's mixed-up feelings were spread out before God.

When Elijah finished his personal confession, God didn't immediately respond to the specific complaint. Instead, He told Elijah to go to the top of the mountain. Those were two things that Elijah was well acquainted with: hearing God say "Go," and climbing to the top of a mountain. So Elijah started climbing.

On the top of Mount Horeb, Elijah waited for God to reveal Himself. But he didn't know how God would come. God had appeared to the Patriarch Job in a whirlwind, to Moses in the fire of a burning bush; at the time of the giving of the Ten Commandments, He had appeared to Moses after a mighty earthquake. With what spectacular accompaniment would He now reveal Himself to Elijah?

First came the wind. Elijah must have clung to a ledge to keep from toppling into a rocky ravine. The rocks themselves catapulted downward in a landslide and broke in pieces. Elijah waited for God to speak, but heard nothing.

Next, and even more frightening, was an earthquake. The rock underneath him shook violently. Huge cracks opened up, swallowing up the wilderness foliage. Elijah waited for God to speak, but heard nothing.

Then a fire broke out. Surely, Elijah thought, God would speak to him from the fire. So he waited, but once again he heard nothing.

Then in the eerie stillness after the wind, earthquake, and fire had ceased, Elijah could faintly hear a soft sound. He listened carefully; it was the sound of a voice, a still small voice, and there was nothing spectacular about it at all.

In the whirlwind, God had given Job a magnificent discourse on the wonders of nature and the magnitude of His creation. At the burning bush God had given Moses a special revelation of Himself as the Great I AM, the God of Abraham, Isaac and Jacob. After the earthquake, God revealed His moral law in the Ten Commandments. But as Elijah listened to the still small voice, all he heard was the same question, "What are you doing here, Elijah?" (19:13) Elijah said, "I have been very zealous for the Lord, the God of hosts; for the sons of Israel have forsaken Thy covenant, torn down Thine altars and killed Thy prophets with the sword. And I alone am left; and they seek my life, to take it away" (19:14).

A Job for Elijah

There are two parts to Elijah's statement. The first expresses his own dedication to the service of God and his dismay with the people of God. The second tells of his solitary position—he alone was left and they were trying to kill him.

God spoke to the first statement, in giving Elijah

something to do. Not something like announcing three years without rain, or fire from heaven, but more commonplace. Elijah had been a prophet of the spectacular; now God wanted him to be a prophet of the ordinary. Usually it is harder to live for God in the ordinariness of daily living than in the excitement of a spiritual revival. Many Christians would be more willing to die for Christ in an arena of lions than they would to live for Christ in the routine of the factory or the humdrum of the home.

God reveals Himself to us not in fireworks, but in quietness. Often He does not reveal Himself through great preachers as much as through our own faithful study of His Word. "Be still [cease striving] and know that I am God," was the instruction that God gave the Psalmist (Ps. 46:10, KJV).

Then God said to Elijah, "Go [there's that word again] to Damascus and anoint Hazael king of Syria. Then anoint Jehu as king of Israel. And finally select Elisha as your successor."

When you are depressed, you feel sorry for yourself and you need to be prodded into activity. Meaningful activity is a good antidote to depression. So God gave Elijah a job. Elijah needed to realize that what happened on Mount Carmel was not the climax of his life. It was not his final victory; there was still more work to be done.

John Simpson, an 18th-century writer, commented: "The prophet was bemoaning the failure of all his efforts to glorify God, and the obstinate determination of his people to continue in their apostasy. It was thus he spent his time in a cave at Horeb, brooding over his disappointment, and lashing himself, by reflecting upon the conduct of the people. A solitary place, with nothing to do, might be congenial with such a disposition; it might foster it, but would never heal it. And this Elijah might have succumbed to a settled melancholy or a raving madness. The only hope for persons in such circumstances is to come out from their lonely haunts, and to be actively employed in some useful and benevolent occupations. This is the best cure for melancholy: to set about doing something which will require muscular exertion, and which will benefit others. Hence God directed Elijah to quit this present lonely abode, which only increased the sadness and irritation of his spirit; and so He gave him a commission to execute a long way off."

One of the main reasons for depression is low self-esteem. If you feel you are worthless and prone to fail, you don't want to try anything. If you feel other people will laugh at you, you will try to avoid contact with others.

But God says, "Get to work anyway." You may think you are worthless, but God doesn't. You may fear what other people think of you, but God says, "Go anyway." And in the going and the doing, you will find new purpose in living.

Rx for Depression

God's formula for handling depression has four ingredients:

1. Get the rest and nourishment your body needs.
2. Talk out your problems; don't keep them bottled up.
3. Wait for God to show Himself to you in a new way.
4. Don't spend your time moping. Do the work God gives to you.

Modern psychology is coming around to recognize

that God's treatment of Elijah was sound. In his book *Depression: What It Is and What to Do About It*, clinical psychologist Roger Barrett gives these tips on treating depression:

1. "Avoid being alone. Depressed people naturally tend to withdraw into themselves and stay away from others. . . . Getting together with others will give them a more realistic perspective on their problems."

2. "Help someone else. Few things will alleviate depression any quicker than finding someone more needy than you are and helping them."

3. Think positively. "The Christian should be able to cut into the vicious circle of negative self-talk. Knowing that God accepts him and considers him of worth and value, he can no longer with integrity bad-mouth himself."

4. Rest in the sovereignty of God. "God is in charge. He is running the universe. God does not expect us to understand the relationship between His sovereignty and this world's happenings, but He does expect us to trust Him."

Work and Fellowship

In Elijah's complaint which he repeated twice to his divine Counselor, there were two parts. The first part had to do with the sinfulness of the people.

To deal with the problem of Part 1, God sent Elijah to anoint three widely disparate people: (1) a pagan king in far-off Syria, 350 miles north; (2) a young man who was currently King Ahab's bodyguard; and (3) a farmboy in Elijah's home territory of Gilead. That motley triumvirate would somehow take care of Ahab, Jezebel, and company. No doubt it seemed unlikely, even to Elijah on Mount Horeb, but he did not argue with God's Word "Go."

(Incidentally, Elijah got around to accomplishing only one of the three, the anointing of the farmboy Elisha to be his successor. You could say that Elisha performed the other two anointings by proxy.)

But Part 2 of Elijah's complaint was "And I, even I only, am left." God couldn't leave that overstatement unchallenged. Elijah had never really accepted Obadiah's claim that there were 100 faithful prophets whom he had hidden in a cave. Elijah felt all alone, as most depressed people do.

But rather than allow Elijah to feel sorry for himself, God said to him, "There are 7,000 others who have not bowed the knee to Baal."

True, 7,000 in an entire nation is still a minority, but it's far more than Elijah had imagined. Perhaps they were not as zealous for Jehovah as Elijah was; perhaps they were not as outspoken in their witness or as bold in their proclamation. Perhaps many of them were like Obadiah, serving in places where Elijah would not imagine a true servant of Jehovah could exist. But in God's reckoning, there were 7,000.

Sometimes we get discouraged by the coldness of our churches or the immoral drift of our nation and we wonder if the faithful can survive. We hear of some who profess to be born again but seem to understand very little what the Gospel is all about. Then we despair.

But God has His 7,000. It is not so many that we can think that the battle can be won by human numbers alone; but it not so few as to make us despair that the true faith will be eradicated from the face of the earth.

God is still sovereign. He is still working in men's hearts, calling people in unlikely places and in unlikely walks of life to Himself.

No, Elijah, the situation is not depressing. In fact, when God is on our side—or should we say, when we are on God's side—there is good reason to celebrate. The victory is assured.

Friends and Enemies: How to Tell Them Apart

9

1 Kings 19:19—21:29

Some things don't go together. Sauerkraut and ice cream, for instance. A tuxedo and swimming trunks. A machine gun in a cathedral. Elijah and Elisha. You might have thought that Elijah and Elisha were nearly identical—that they dressed alike, talked alike, and ate the same brand of grasshoppers for dinner. Not so.

Even though their names are similar and they both came from Gilead, they were so different that you wonder how they ever got along with each other.

God provides us with some strange match-ups at times—church friends and neighbors with whom we feel so incompatible. We chafe in the companionship; we endure it, rather than enjoy it.

If you have ever experienced one of God's incongruous match-ups, maybe there is something you can learn from the way that Elijah and Elisha complemented each other.

It may be a neighbor next door to you; it may be a co-worker in the office; it could even be a brother or sister; yes, it could even be a husband or wife. But whoever it is, you have cause to question what purpose God can possibly have in it. You say, "Lord, I know I have to accept the fact that You put me here alongside this person, but at the moment I can't think of a single good thing that can come from our association together."

A Prophet Employed

To understand Elijah's situation better, let's return to the story. After God spoke to Elijah on Mount Horeb, the prophet dutifully headed north. Two months had passed since the drought had subsided. Elijah, realizing that he was still a marked man and that Queen Jezebel's henchmen could arrest him at any moment, probably avoided the major cities of Judah and Israel and took detours around areas where Ahab would maintain a strong military presence.

But this wasn't the same Elijah that had run pell-mell into the wilderness. Something was different. Now he had a job to do. He felt useful again. No longer did he regard himself an utter failure. As long as Jehovah wanted to use him in His service, Elijah knew he had a purpose in living. He was no longer in the ranks of the unemployed, and it felt good.

That was another point. As long as there was a job for him to do, he had confidence that Jehovah would help him do it. Old King Ahab couldn't stop him. After all, God had commissioned him to anoint Ahab's successor and that meant Ahab was a lame duck, living on borrowed time. Although he didn't know it, his reign was coming to an end.

As he hiked out of the wilderness through the Negev, into Judah, and then into his homeland of Israel, he saw the farmers and shepherds out in the fields. The pastures were green now, not parched as they were two months earlier.

To the Meadow of Dancing

Where was Elijah going? He was on his way to find a man named Elisha, the son of Shaphat who lived in a town called Abelmeholah. This was one of three tasks that God had assigned to him, but finding Elisha was probably the simplest of the three. There is no reason to assume that Elijah knew Elisha earlier in life, although as something of a traveler, Elijah probably had passed through Elisha's home town of Abelmeholah. (Scholars today are not as sure of the location of Abelmeholah as Elijah was, although most of them think it was in the fertile Jordan Valley about halfway between the Sea of Galilee and the Dead Sea.)

In Abelmeholah, which literally means "the meadow of dancing," Elijah was to find his successor. That must have seemed like a strange place to find a new prophet. Besides that, Elisha was a rich boy. His father, Shaphat (which means judge), had 12 yoke of oxen, which is a sure sign that he was well-to-do. Can you imagine the running conversation that Elijah must have had with the Lord as he spotted Elisha in the field?

"First of all, Lord, I'm not sure about this whole idea of anointing my own successor. You know, I haven't reached retirement age yet. When I said I wanted to quit, I wasn't myself. Now that I've had a good rest and can see things a little more clearly, I don't think You should be too hasty about finding my replacement."

On Mount Horeb, when Elijah was depressed, God had handled his case with divine wisdom. It was good that God commissioned him to go back to work again; it was good that God commanded him to become involved with people. But why did God give to Elijah the traumatic experience of finding his own successor?

I think that it was to show Elijah that his work wasn't a failure. Let me explain. You need a successor only if you have started something that needs to be perpetuated. George Washington wouldn't have needed a successor if the nation had collapsed during his two terms in the presidency. But because he had succeeded, he needed a successor.

So the experience of finding Elisha was designed to be an encouragement to Elijah. "Elijah," God might have told him, "I'm going to continue what I've started through you. You may think that you've been a failure. After all, Ahab is still up to his old tricks. But remember, Elijah, I'm in charge. And even if ultimate success isn't achieved in your lifetime, I will see that victory will come. That's why you need a successor."

I think God had other reasons too. Elijah needed fellowship, just as every Christian does. He may have felt that life was easier without people, but God knew he needed them anyway. If Elisha was going to be his successor, it was logical that he would have to learn the ropes from Elijah. That meant they would need to spend a great deal of time with each other.

Together Elijah and Elisha were able to do things that they couldn't have done separately. For one thing they were able to revive a school for prophets. It wasn't anything like our theological seminaries, because they didn't have an established curriculum and they didn't graduate with a degree, but still you could liken Elijah to the president and Elisha to the dean of students.

The Heir Apparent

Of course, when Elijah was looking down the furrows in Elisha's plowed fields, he didn't understand all of God's reasons. Instead, he might have been thinking: "Lord, if You really think I need a successor, I can think of better places to find one than the 'meadow of dancing' and more likely prospects than the son of a rich farmer."

And he might have been thinking: "Where was Elisha when I was being fed by ravens at the Brook Cherith? Where was Elisha when I was holed up in Zarephath? Where indeed?"

Elisha and his wealthy father with the fertile farmland in the Jordan Valley were among those who were least affected by the three-year drought. Yet there could be no doubt that Elisha was the one who had been chosen by the Lord. So the prophet trekked across the furrows to meet the heir apparent.

When explorer Henry Stanley met missionary David Livingstone in darkest Africa, he simply said, "Dr. Livingstone, I presume." But, it would seem, Elijah had less to say to Elisha than that. Elijah, as you know, was not a man of many words. Instead, he took his shaggy cloak and flung it over the shoulders of the last plowman in the line of 12 plowmen who were cultivating the field. That last plowman was Elisha.

What an odd couple they were! One rich, one poor. One of wealthy parents, one whose parents were unknown. One settled, one a wanderer. One outgoing, one introverted. One a farmer, one whose occupation was unknown.

The Bible says simply: "Elijah passed over to him and threw his mantle on him" (19:19). (The mantle was probably a goatskin cloak.) The symbolism may seem strange to us, but to both Elijah and Elisha there was no doubt what it meant. It was like an orchestra conductor passing his baton to his successor or a judge handing his gavel to his replacement. It symbolized the eventual transfer of power.

But there was more to it than merely turning over the reins of prophetic leadership. Discipleship must precede leadership. But Elijah may not have been thinking of Elisha as his disciple—only as his successor. So Elijah walked past Elisha across the field, and the young farmer had to chase after him. In the New Testament, Jesus called His disciples to follow Him, and in obedience to His call they left their fishing nets and followed Him. Even though Elisha hadn't been summoned by Elijah to follow, he did so anyway.

First, he asked permission to say good-bye to his parents. Next, in a striking symbolic act, he slaughtered a yoke of oxen, boiled the meat and served it to the people of the community. Not only did this symbolize a clear-cut break with his life as a farmer, but it also identified the people in his future calling. The die was cast, there was no backing down on his commitment now.

Afterward, Elisha went with Elijah and "ministered unto him." Exactly how he ministered is unknown, but it seems he became Elijah's servant. Second Kings 3:11 identifies Elisha as the one who "poured water on the hands of Elijah." That's almost unbelievable.

God Chose Elisha

Obviously, God had been working in Elisha's life preparing him for this day. To forsake the role of being a gentleman farmer and instead adopt a position of a servant of a hunted itinerant prophet of Jehovah is not what the vocational counselor at the local prep school would have advised.

I don't know about you, but I think I would have been tempted to tell my parents, "Elijah has chosen me, but I'm not sure it's going to work out. So keep a spare bedroom available, just in case." I'm afraid that's the way we often respond to the Lord's call today.

If you were Elisha's mom or dad, how do you think you would have responded to the exciting news that your son was going to forsake the family fortune and follow a man on King Ahab's Wanted List? Elisha's mother and father must have been exceptional people.

Elisha killed the oxen and invited all his neighborhood friends to become witnesses of his decisive action, by partaking of the flesh. Then he became Elijah's follower, even though Elijah didn't seem to want a follower.

That's Elijah for you. And that's the way I sometimes am. I don't mind contacts with people as long as they don't get in my way, as long as they don't impose on me, as long as I'm not inconvenienced. I like to choose my friends and not have friendships forced upon me.

Are you like that too? That may be one reason why we sometimes find it difficult to establish true friendships with relatives. We like to choose our friends, but we can't choose our relatives.

Jesus told His disciples, "I have called you friends," and as they became friends of Jesus, they became friends of one another as well. Indeed, it was only because of divine love that such a motley bunch of fishermen, tax collectors, zealots and others could be transformed into a cohesive fellowship.

The early church in Antioch is another example of unlikely people being united in Christian fellowship. The Holy Spirit made that conglomeration into a model for Christian missionary activity.

Whenever God imposes friends upon us whom we wouldn't choose for ourselves, it's tempting to pack up and move to another church or community. But God might have much to teach us through such associations, even as He had much to teach the "odd couple," Elijah and Elisha.

A 10-Year Hiatus

The Bible doesn't go into any details about what happened during the next 10 years of their lives. Apparently, the two worked together in a master-servant relationship. Much of their ministry may have been mundane. Certainly it didn't rival the suspenseful, spine-tingling moments of Elijah's summit conference on Mount Carmel.

A. W. Pink speculates on the missing years this way: "We may be sure they redeemed the time. Probably in distant parts of the land they sought to instruct the people in the worship of Jehovah, opposing the prevailing idolatry and general corruption, laboring diligently though quietly to effect a solid reformation. It would seem that, following the example of Samuel, they established schools here and there for fitting young men unto the prophetic office, instructing them in the knowledge of God's law and preparing them to become expounders of it unto the people."

Fortunately for Elijah and Elisha, King Ahab was engaged in warfare against Syria during much of this period, so he didn't have the inclination or the troops to chase after a couple of itinerant prophets in the hinterlands of his own nation. This allowed Elijah and Elisha the freedom to preach, teach, and train. But there is one major story during the 10-year hiatus where Elijah surfaced again. It's a story with three main characters: a landowner in Israel named Naboth, King Ahab, and the prophet Elijah.

Naboth's Vineyard

Next to Ahab's winter palace in Jezreel was a vineyard owned by Naboth. King Ahab wanted it for an herb garden and he made a business proposition to Naboth that seemed fair enough. He offered Naboth a better vineyard in another part of Israel or else a fair price.

Naboth nixed the deal. On the surface it looked like poor manners, not to say poor politics, to turn thumbs down on a deal with the king. But the problem was that under Israelite law (see Num. 27:8-11), Naboth was prohibited from selling the land. According to the law, he was technically not the owner of the land but a steward. The land had belonged to his father and grandfather as well as to his children and grandchildren. It had been entrusted to his family line by God. As a result, Naboth rightly felt he could not give the title of the land to anyone else, and that included King Ahab.

Well, Ahab went home and sulked, in a not very kingly way. He went to bed and refused to eat, which is exactly what little children do when they don't get their way.

Enter Queen Jezebel. She didn't see why her husband needed to sulk. After all, wasn't he the king? Couldn't he do whatever he wanted to? As a Gentile, she didn't value the importance of the Mosaic Law. Even if she had understood the Laws of Moses, it wouldn't have made any difference to her. All she knew was that no peasant should frustrate a king.

So she devised a plan. In the town of Jezreel a fast was proclaimed. Any time a fast was proclaimed, it indicated that a major civil crime had been committed, either by the community as a whole or by certain individuals within the community.

At a feast, it was a mark of honor to be placed in front of the people. But at a fast, it was a mark of dishonor. Under orders of Queen Jezebel, Naboth was placed in front and false witnesses testified against him to make his arrest appear legal.

Jezebel's plan worked perfectly. Naboth was stoned to death, his murder meeting the legal standards of Mosaic Law. Best of all from Jezebel's point of view, Ahab was not implicated in the stoning. Wasn't she shrewd?

Since Naboth's sons were stoned with him (see 2 Kings 9:26), Ahab quickly moved in to take possession of the vineyard he had coveted. It was the right of the crown to take possession of property when there was no heir. Everything was very legal and proper.

But the next day when Ahab went to Naboth's vineyard, he found an unexpected intruder. It was Elijah, and he wasn't there to buy grapes. Though they hadn't seen each other for several years, the king recognized Elijah immediately. "Have you found me, O my enemy?" the king asked.

The last time they had met, Ahab had asked, "Is this you, you troubler of Israel?" He had identified Elijah as the troubler of the nation at that time, but now his accusation was personal. Elijah was now the troubler of the king; he was the enemy.

The last time they had met, Ahab felt that he had found Elijah; this time Ahab realized that Elijah had found him. In spite of the fact of Jezebel's vow to slay Elijah—and the prophet had every reason to avoid a confrontation with the king and queen—King Ahab knew that, in this divine game of tag, he was "it." The prophet of Jehovah had found him. He was the one with the guilty conscience. No matter how legal and proper it looked to outsiders, Ahab carried a weight of guilt on his royal shoulders. Like Adam in Eden, the man with the load of guilt is a man in hiding. However, hiding is futile in such a game, for there is no place that the eye of God cannot see.

"Where can I flee from Thy presence?" asked the psalmist (Ps. 139:7). As he probed the most inaccessible place of the universe, he confessed that there was no hiding place from God. King David could find great comfort in the thought that he could not elude the all-seeing eye of God. But there was no comfort in the thought for King Ahab. It made Ahab panic.

From personal experience, King David had learned that as long as God has 20/20 vision, there is no such thing as a perfect crime. David had Uriah killed to gain his wife Bathsheba. Just as Elijah had come to Ahab, so the prophet Nathan had come to David. Even the careful schemes of kings do not fool God. You are always a loser when you try to put something over on God.

Power by Intimidation

In recent years, a new rash of books has been published on the subjects "Power," "Aggression," "Manipulation," "Intimidation." These books pull no punches. They are blatant, making no bones about their me-first approach. It's the survival of the fittest. The philosophy is selfishness, pure and simple.

This was exactly the philosophy of King Ahab. People were objects to be used; they were not humans to be honored. As a result, Naboth's vineyard was more important to Ahab than Naboth. The acquisition of things to gratify his own pleasure was more important than the friendship of people.

It was precisely to keep the Ahabs of the world from seizing all the property from the Naboths that God had established His Old Testament Laws. The Law declared, "The land, moreover, shall not be sold permanently, for the land is Mine" (Lev. 25:23). And again, "The sons of Israel shall each hold to the inheritance of the tribe of his fathers" (Num 36:7).

Whenever we succumb to the rat race of amassing things, people shrink in size. Soon they become mere chess pieces to be sacrificed so that we can achieve our ambition.

This is how slavery could maintain its hold in a nation with a strong Christian heritage. This is how some Christian businessmen today can amass fortunes at the expense of their employees. This is how even Sunday School contests and soul-winning campaigns can be subverted.

Power-hungry Ahabs are just as much idolators as Baal-worshiping Jezebels. They may think they are indifferent to religion, but nevertheless they are slavishly worshiping a materialistic god.

Maybe even deeper than that is another problem. On one level, you could say that Ahab's god was materialism, but on a deeper level, you see clearly that Ahab had another god—himself. He was worshiping a god made in his own image and self-centered, he sulked when he didn't get his own way. Nothing was more important than giving himself what he wanted.

That is the philosophy of the current plethora of books on power, aggression and intimidation. Be your own god, make up your own laws as you go, satisfy yourself, gratify your own pleasures, serve yourself.

But remember, the man who did that in biblical times was an enemy of Elijah, the servant of God. Like the barn-building farmer of Luke 12 who laid up treasure for himself, his doom was pronounced. Earth treasure is always a short-term investment.

The Price of a Man

The enemy of Ahab declared, "I have found you, because you have sold yourself to do evil in the sight of the Lord" (21:20).

Ahab wasn't the first rich man who sold himself, nor was he the last; they still do it today. It sounds like a poor bargain for a king to sell himself for a vineyard, but men sell themselves for less. Perhaps the true worth of a man is measured not in what he possesses, but in the price for which he is willing to sell himself. In George Eliot's novel, Silas Marner sold himself for his pile of gold. In *The Devil and Daniel Webster,* a New England farmer sold his soul for prosperity on his farm. Hollywood starlets sell themselves for fame; politicians sell themselves for position; businessmen sell themselves for power.

E. M. Blaiklock of New Zealand says, "We can have what we want at a price. Peace and joy are the first installment in such retribution. 'The joy of the godless is but for a moment,' said Job."

Certainly Ahab's joy was but for a moment. He had pictured turning Naboth's vineyard into a lovely herb garden. Now that dream was on the verge of becoming a reality. He was overjoyed, enthusiastic, buoyant.

Then came his old nemesis, Elijah, the man who had brought him a three-year drought. Before Elijah got through with the king, he had predicted utter destruction not only on Ahab and Jezebel, but also upon their dynasty (21:21-24). Ahab's joy was literally "but for a moment." No doubt, he would have preferred another three-year drought.

While the sentence of doom was temporarily stayed by Ahab's repentance, yet there was another man in Naboth's vineyard that day who was to fulfill Elijah's prophecy. Riding behind Ahab's royal chariot was a young military officer, an aide to the king, by the name of Jehu. The events in Naboth's vineyard were etched deeply in his mind. It was almost as if God had put a posthypnotic suggestion into Jehu's mind; 20 years later, Jehu responded violently to wipe out all traces of Ahab's descendents. (For the bloody details, see 2 Kings 4.)

All that fuss over a vineyard? Why in the world would the Lord want to make a federal case out of that? After all, Ahab wasn't going to turn it into a brothel or a temple of Baal. He was merely going to change it into a little herb garden, or as the newer translations put it, a vegetable garden. What does God have against vegetable gardens?

Nothing at all. But even good things can be corrupted by doing them in evil ways. The end does not justify the means. Sometimes we forget that. Like Ahab, we see a vineyard out of our window. "If only I had that vineyard, what I would do with it! Why I would cut down all the vines and transform it into a beautiful vegetable garden." Nothing wrong with that, is there?

Then step two: "You know, I really should have that vineyard. It looks quite ugly next to my palace. It's decreasing my property value."

Step three: "I'll be a nice fellow. I'll make Mr.

Naboth a generous offer, one he can't refuse. Besides, he wouldn't dare refuse the king."

Step four: "Why that impudent, inconsiderate, unpatriotic ingrate. He can't do that to me. Doesn't he know who I am? He must be a Communist or something. It's his patriotic duty to sell me that property."

Step five: "Obviously, there's only one thing to do, even my wife says so. Naboth's got to go; for the good of the whole nation, to say nothing of myself."

Although we hate to admit it, we rationalize our actions in the same way. We can even make it appear to be the Lord's will by the time we get to step five.

Ahab violated at least three of the Ten Commandments in the process of going from steps one to five. Throughout history, some of the vilest acts have been done in the name of Christianity. The Crusades are one case in point. Christians often forget to be Christian and run roughshod over friend and foe alike to accomplish their goals. But there is always an Elijah in the shadows to spoil our fun. When he comes, we with our twisted values think he is the enemy.

"Sin," says E. M. Blaiklock, "is desiring good things selfishly, with no thought for another, at the wrong time, at the wrong place, and in defiance of God's law." No doubt the last major squabble in your church would be another case in point.

Ahab Sold Himself

Compare Ahab and Elisha for a moment. Ahab is the example of the modern man who uses power to abuse people. He is the ruthless man who gets what he wants, only to find an Elijah in his vineyard.

Elisha is the example of a man who had everything,

but who was willing to give it up in order to be a servant. He became a friend of a friendless prophet and helped to nurse him back to a strong mental and emotional state again. He was a co-worker, working with the servants on his father's farm, with Elijah, and with the schools of prophets established throughout the land.

Elisha was more interested in people than power. But God gave him power too. It was Elisha who anointed the two heads of state (Hazael in Syria and Jehu in Israel). And it was Elisha to whom the commanding general of the Syrian army came when he sought a cure for his leprosy. Are you looking for a way to win friends and influence people? Then follow Elisha's example.

As for Ahab, three years after he was confronted by Elijah in the vineyard, he was struck by a chance arrow in battle, thus ending a turbulent 22-year reign.

The Bible speaks of Ahab's accomplishment of having built an ivory house (22:39), which has recently been unearthed by archeologists. No doubt it was a marvel to behold. So don't write Ahab off as a mere nothing. He was a man of power and influence. After all, isn't that the reason why he married Jezebel? So he could have more power and influence?

He knew how to make an impression on others too. He knew how to sell himself. In fact, he was so successful in selling himself to Jezebel that she bought him and owned him.

The Bible's final note on Ahab is, "Surely there was no one like Ahab who sold himself to do evil in the sight of the Lord, because Jezebel his wife incited him" (21:25).

It Isn't Much, but It's All I've Got

10

1 Kings 16:29—17:1

If you've been successful in identifying with Elijah thus far, you'll appreciate these two stories, although they may present you with a challenge.

In the first, soldiers came to capture the prophet and he fought them with fire from heaven. More soldiers were sent by the king and they too went up in flames.

In the second, Elijah and Elisha took a walk together, and a whirlwind came along and escorted Elijah to heaven.

How can any normal 20th-century human being get anything practical from those fantastic stories? Not only are they difficult to identify with; they are also hard to believe.

Fire for Samaria

Interestingly enough, though we may have difficulty with them, the disciples in the New Testament didn't. They felt they could identify with Elijah and apply the message of these stories to their lives.

Here's the way it happened. A village in Samaria wasn't very hospitable to Jesus and His disciples as they headed southward to attend a feast in Jerusalem. Samaritans had a strange quirk. They could be fairly civil to you if you were headed away from Jerusalem, but they would do anything they could to make it difficult for you to pass through their territory if you were going the other way.

Well, some of the disciples had recently been on the Mount of Transfiguration where they had witnessed their Master talking with Moses and Elijah. Apparently the disciples were too much in shock to comprehend everything, but they did hear Jesus mention that He would soon be leaving them. They must have wondered if Jesus would be taken up to heaven as Elijah was.

Then came the rejection by the Samaritans. Since it was in Samaria, 875 years earlier, that Elijah had called fire from heaven to consume the king's soldiers, Christ's disciples put two and two together and decided that these Samaritans who rejected the Messiah should be accorded at least as drastic punishment as those who had rejected Elijah.

"Shall we call down fire from heaven?" asked James and John, who hadn't been given the nickname "Sons of Thunder" for nothing. Obviously, they were seeking to apply Scripture to a relevant situation, and Elijah was very much on their minds. But instead of praising them for being such astute Bible students, Jesus rebuked them. God's kingdom is not advanced by burning people with fire.

God Is Righteous

How is it possible for us to apply the first chapter of 2 Kings? Part of the answer comes from what John the

Baptist said: "The Law was given through Moses; grace and truth were realized through Jesus Christ" (John 1:17). The Law given at Mount Sinai reminds us of God's righteousness and holiness. Elijah, who also received his vision of God at Mount Sinai, was following in Moses' footsteps.

But there is more to God than the Law. On a mount called Calvary, Jesus supremely revealed a heavenly Father with a heart of love and mercy. That's why Jesus forbade James and John to invoke judgment on those rude Samaritans.

Sometimes we forget the vision of God that Elijah had. If we think of God as cotton candy—full of fluff and sugary sweet—sin doesn't look so bad and the state of the unsaved doesn't perturb us. We even begin to smile at the little foibles in our own life that we used to call iniquity. So it's good for us to be reminded of a God whose holiness and righteousness are so crystal pure that sin is abhorrent. Then idolatry, whether it is Baal worship or the kind that is practiced in our neighborhoods today, deserves to be punished.

The Bible's complete view of God as righteous, just, loving, and merciful, is one that should shape our actions day by day. On the multiple choice tests that you used to take in school, you had the opportunity to check a, b, c, d, none of the above, or all of the above. When it comes to describing God, unless you answer "all of the above," your answer is wrong. God is (a) righteous, (b) just, (c) loving and (d) merciful, all four and even more.

However, the big lesson to be learned from 2 Kings 1 and 2 is not the lesson of subtraction (How many soldiers were killed?) but rather the lesson of multiplication. Let me explain.

Ahaziah

The story of Elijah is basically the struggle between a prophet and a king. God was teaching Elijah to multiply righteousness, King Ahab was doing a good job of multiplying unrighteousness.

Ahab's son Ahaziah was on the throne, (see 1 Kings 22:51; 2 Kings 1:2) and he was a carbon copy of his father. Interestingly enough, Ahaziah's name means "Jehovah has ahold," or in the terms of the old spiritual, "He's got you and me, brother, in His hands." Strange that Ahab should give his son a name that spoke of the power and sovereignty of Jehovah. Yet it's a further indication that Ahab vacillated between Jehovah and Baal, trying to play both sides of the street.

Ahaziah, who took the throne about 851 B.C., had a short and dismal reign. The first verse of 2 Kings tells of the rebellion of Moab against Ahaziah. About 100 years ago, archeologists found the famous Moabite Stone which tells the story. In the latter years of Ahab's reign, his troops were so concerned about the Syrian menace in the northeast that they neglected the rumblings of the Moabite guerrilla forces in the southeast. Since Jezebel's father ruled Sidon to the northwest, that front was peaceful. When Ahab died, the Moabites saw their chance to break their yoke completely. Ahab's successor, Ahaziah, was young and untried. No doubt they thought he would not be able to take bold action against them immediately. They were right, but not for the reasons they thought.

Lord of the Flies

Ahaziah must have been pacing his rooftop, which is where people in those days went when they wanted to pace floors. Either he forgot to stop when he got to the end of the rooftop or he paused to lean against the railing which collapsed, plummeting Ahaziah to the ground.

Critically injured, Ahaziah sent messengers to the Philistine town of Ekron to inquire of Baalzebub if he would recover. *Baalzebub* literally means "lord of the flies," and it is possible that this god was a local deity specializing in health and disease cures. Since flies bore disease, it seemed logical to call on the lord of the flies to overcome the disease.

Many scholars think, however, that the name was really *Baal-zebul*, "lord of the high place," and that the Hebrews, whose humor was often sarcastic, had derisively nicknamed the deity Baalzebub, lord of the flies, as a joke.

Regardless of the true meaning of the name, King Ahaziah thought he could find help from the ancient Philistine shrine at Ekron. But before the messengers got to Ekron, they were met by a strange looking man who told them that their ruler would die. When they returned and described the man to Ahaziah, there was no doubt in his mind that the man was Elijah. It had to be.

Angered, Ahaziah sent a captain and 50 soldiers to capture Elijah, the longtime nemesis of his father. When the captain approached Elijah's abode, he ordered him, with military authority, to accompany him back to the king's palace.

The captain's orders came from King Ahaziah, but Elijah obeyed a higher authority. The captain said, "Thou man of God, the king has said, 'Come down.'"

Elijah, however, was not one of the king's "flunkies." So he responded, "If I be a man of God, let fire come down from heaven." The Hebrew word for man is *ish* and for fire is *esh*. Elijah's response was a play on words, but the audience didn't enjoy Elijah's pun. The captain and his 50 men were incinerated.

Ahaziah was a slow learner. He thought that what had happened was a freak lightning storm, and so he sent another captain with his company. Once again the incident was repeated. Lightning struck twice in the same place, according to the reports that Ahaziah received back at the palace.

When a third captain confronted Elijah, the scene could have been done in triplicate, except for the fact that this captain asked Elijah for mercy. So Elijah obliged and accompanied him to the king's palace, where he took the opportunity to repeat God's message directly to Ahaziah.

A few years earlier, Elijah had run in terror when Jezebel threatened to kill him. Now, surrounded by a troop of armed men, he did not fear. He had learned the lesson that David had sung about: "For by Thee I can run upon a troop. . . . He is a shield to all who take refuge in Him" (2 Sam. 22:30-31).

Ahab's Family

Once again, Elijah's integrity as a prophet was proven. As Elijah predicted, Ahaziah soon died, after a reign of only two years. The Bible says, "And he did evil in the sight of the Lord, and walked in the way of his father and in the way of his mother. . . . he served Baal and worshiped him" (1 Kings 22:52-53).

But Ahaziah wasn't the only offspring of Ahab and Jezebel to sit on the throne. Succeeding Ahaziah as king was his younger brother Jehoram, since Ahaziah had died before he had any children to take his place on the throne. Ahaziah's sister, Athaliah, married the king of Judah to the south. Her husband reigned over Judah for seven years; then one of her sons took over as king for one year; and she herself succeeded her son as ruling monarch for six years.

Now I don't expect you to remember all of that, but you should remember a couple of things. Here was a family of kings and queens. Within a dozen years, Ahab, two of his sons, one of his daughters, a son-in-law and a grandson had all been ruling monarchs.

Not bad for one family? Yes, it was bad, as bad as bad can be. It was triply tragic that Ahab had the gall to put the name of Jehovah into the names of the three children who became kings and queens. They may have borne the name of Jehovah, but they worshiped Baal.

Ahab multiplied evil. Not even a computer could multiply evil faster than Ahab. Yet, as I read the biblical account, I feel a bit sorry for old Ahab. As a monarch, he seemed able enough. Politically, he was quite astute. But because he worshiped power, he became morally bankrupt.

Owen Whitehouse, a 19th-century British scholar, commented, "It is more than doubtful whether Ahab really comprehended the religious issues."

Perhaps not. But that does not excuse him. If he saw everything in terms of politics instead of morality and religion, does that reduce his spiritual liability? Not at all.

In spite of the fact that Queen Jezebel could manipulate him in any direction that she wanted him to go, King Ahab was one of the abler kings in the history of Israel.

Multiplier of Evil

What then went wrong? Why did a man of ability degenerate into a multiplier of evil?

1. The problem can be traced to his desire for political power. This overshadowed all other considerations in his life. This was why his wedding with Jezebel was arranged. This was also why Baal worship was introduced into Israel.

Baal worship was tied into Ahab's mind-set, for it too was essentially the worship of power. Morality and righteousness were not considered in Baal worship. You worshiped Baal because you feared his power. He might destroy you if you didn't.

Contrast that with the worship of Jehovah. In one of the psalms David wrote, "The righteous Lord loveth righteousness" (Ps. 11:7, KJV). In the New Testament Jesus taught His disciples to pray, "Our Father who art in heaven, hallowed (holy) be Thy name" (Matt. 6:9).

People are always transformed into the image of the god they worship. Because Baal worship regarded righteousness as irrelevant, Ahab soon regarded it as irrelevant too. It really didn't matter as long as he had power.

At first, that doesn't seem to apply to our lives. It seems long ago and far away. After all, when was the last time you saw an image of Baal perched in the backyard of one of your neighbors? But practically speaking, you may find good reason to examine what you and your family really worship.

If you were to ask the members of your family to rate (from one to ten) what is really of most importance to them, how far down the ladder would righteousness be?

If those same things were rated on the basis of the amount of time you devoted to cultivating and developing them, would that improve or decrease the ranking of righteousness?

The point is, you can multiply unrighteousness in the lives of your family members simply by giving God less importance than you give to other people and things.

2. Something else contributed to Ahab's ability to multiply evil. It was this: he disparaged God's servants. Through much of his reign, it was outright persecution.

Little wonder then that Ahaziah thought he could order Elijah down from the mountain. Little wonder that Ahab's grandchildren vandalized the house of God in Jerusalem (2 Chron. 24:7).

God's servants are not to be taken lightly. Of course, they are human and they make mistakes. Sometimes they may be deserving of public censure. But the family that makes it a practice to minimize the servants that God is using may find that they will reap in their children the same disrespect for men of God that Ahab passed along to his descendents.

3. A third factor that contributed to the evil heritage that Ahab gave his children was his habit of disregarding God's judgments. Neither Ahab nor Ahaziah recognized a judgment of God when they saw one.

Apparently Ahab never really got God's message about the three-year drought in his country. Though the message should have been clear enough, especially with Elijah underlining the key words, Ahab— political animal that he was—could only understand messages from kingdoms below and not from the King above. Because he didn't take sin seriously, he didn't respect God's judgments. Or else, he just chose to totally ignore them.

That's why Ahaziah didn't realize what was happening to his troops when they were destroyed by fire.

He had seen his father ignore God's judgments so often that he had acquired the habit himself.

In our day, when we seldom see people destroyed by God's judgment, it is easy for us to play games with God and to take His judgments lightly. But it is no less dangerous than for Ahaziah. God has not changed. He is not fooled by our playing games with Him. The prophet Malachi warned the Israelites about the danger of trifling with God. In his day they were bringing blind and sick lambs to offer as sacrifices to God, instead of lambs without blemish and without spot as God had commanded. Through Malachi, the message came to the people, "For I, the Lord, do not change. . . . You are cursed with a curse, for you are robbing Me, the whole nation of you!" (Mal. 3:6, 9)

Those three things: (1) confused priorities, (2) disparagement of God's servants, and (3) playing games with God's judgment, fostered the evil that was passed along in Ahab's royal line.

Multiplier of Good

While Ahab was multiplying evil, Elijah was learning how to multiply good. That's another story, told in 2 Kings 2.

It's a strange story, beginning with Elijah telling his right-hand man Elisha to stay in the town of Gilgal while He went to the town of Bethel. Elisha, normally an obedient helper to Elijah, said No; he would stay with him. If Elijah was going to Bethel, Elisha was not about to stay in Gilgal alone.

In Bethel the two were met by the students at the Bethel School of the Prophets. The Living Bible tells the story like this, in its typical colloquial fashion: "The young prophets of Bethel Seminary came out to meet them and asked Elisha, 'Did you know that the Lord is going to take Elijah away from you today?'

"'Quiet,' Elisha snapped. 'Of course, I know it.'"

Well, that explains why Elisha didn't want to leave the side of Elijah on this particular day. Something big was going to happen. He had been Elijah's understudy for eight to ten years, and he certainly didn't want to miss Elijah's final performance.

Perhaps Elijah didn't hear the young prophets talking with Elisha. At any rate, once again he tried to elude Elisha. This time Elijah was headed toward Jericho where there was another branch of the school of the prophets.

These prophets also told Elisha what he already knew. From Jericho, Elijah headed to the Jordan River and once again urged Elisha to stay with the younger prophets. But not for the world would Elisha miss the last act.

From a distance the student prophets watched their two leaders approach the Jordan River. Then they saw Elijah take his cloak, fold it up and strike the water with it. Miraculously a path opened through the river and Elijah and Elisha crossed to the other side.

Across the Jordan, Elijah asked Elisha if there was anything that he wanted and Elisha responded, "'Please let a double portion of your spirit be upon me'" (2 Kings 2:9). Elijah said that his wish would be granted if Elisha would witness his departure from the world.

The two walked a bit farther and "as they were going along and talking there appeared a chariot of fire and horses of fire which separated the two of them. And Elijah went up by a whirlwind to heaven" (2:11).

Elijah's Legacy

Remember how the story of Elijah began? A solitary figure, a man out of nowhere, confronting big, bad King Ahab.

Remember how the story of Elijah reached its climax? A solitary figure on top of Mount Carmel, confronting the prophets of Baal and calling down fire from heaven.

Remember how the story of Elijah continued? A solitary figure on top of Mount Horeb, bemoaning his fate to God: "I, even I only, am left."

Now look at this final scene from Elijah's life. His great final victory is not that he left this earthly existence in a whirlwind; his final victory is that he left two or three schools of prophets, plus a well-trained assistant to carry on his work.

You may be impressed with God's miracle in taking Elijah to heaven in a whirlwind. Personally, I am more impressed with God's miracle of making Elijah, the solitary figure on the mountain, into a molder of men. In this way, God used Elijah to multiply godliness.

A Teacher of Teachers

Many great men are individualists, as Elijah was. Their exploits may be spectacular. But they become greater when they learn to reach and teach others.

The Apostle Paul, early in his life, was a headstrong individualist. But God taught him that there was a more effective way to spread the Gospel. Paul was not a team player when he started out. The first missionary team consisted of Paul, Barnabas, and Mark, but the team fell apart before their first term was over. Yet, when Paul wrote his final epistle, he told Timothy, who had been his Elisha for many years,

"The things you heard me say in the presence of many witnesses entrust to reliable men who will also be qualified to teach others" (2 Tim. 2:2, NIV).

In other words, the most effective way to spread godliness is by sharing it with others to such an extent that they in turn will be able to pass it along to still another generation.

This is what Elijah did. He trained Elisha, who in turn trained the various schools of prophets who became equipped to teach the people.

If you are a parent, the message you should gain from this is not only that you should teach your children the Word of God and set a godly example for them. The message is also that you should prepare them to be teachers so that they can share God's Word with their peers and live godly lives with their companions. That isn't always easy. But it takes the worry out of parenting.

If your children get their Christian beliefs from you by osmosis, they will keep them as long as they stay close to you. However, when they become close to others, they will start to imbibe the thinking of their nearest and most persuasive companion. If, on the other hand, they are instructed to become sharers themselves, then the tendency will be for them to lead others rather than to be led by others.

Schools for Prophets

If as much space were devoted to the latter part of Elijah's ministry as is given to his earlier years, you would need a separate book of the Bible called Elijah. While little is said about these years, it seems obvious that Elijah, accompanied by his management trainee Elisha, spent much time developing schools for prophets. The man who bemoaned the fact that he was standing alone and that all his countrymen had bowed the knee to Baal was now being made to eat his words. Not only were there many (God said there were 7,000) who hadn't worshiped the Phoenician deity, but Elijah was given the task of training many of the young men to take up where he had left off.

I wouldn't be at all surprised if some of these older prophets were from the 100 that Obadiah had kept alive in a cave during the three-year drought.

What is a Prophet?

As we use the word *prophet,* we usually think of a fellow with a crystal ball who can tell you what's going to happen in the future. But that's not the biblical definition. Simply put, a biblical prophet was a man who spoke to men the words of God.

Yet there's more to it than that. The biblical prophet was one who understood the flow of history, from God's point of view. This gave him a perspective not only of the past and the present but also of the future.

That precisely is the way that Elijah emerged as a true prophet. Understanding how God had worked in the past, he could predict a drought for the future.

Sometimes God spoke by direct revelation to these prophets, but not always. While prediction played a part in the ministries of most prophets, proclamation played a much bigger role. In the ministry of Elijah it seemed about 90 percent proclamation and 10 percent prediction.

But the key was that the prophets could tell you the meaning of current events. They were the TV news analysts of their day.

F. B. Meyer says that the original word for prophet means "bubbling over." Meyer said, "Elijah was a spiritual geyser, the mouthpiece and spokesman of God."

God calls us all to be spiritual geysers, bubbling over with the Word of God. Christianity is not a one-man show. It is not a game where we applaud the minister. We are all called to be God's spiritual geysers, activating others as we go.

Elijah's ministry began with his personal testimony before King Ahab. He affirmed the meaning of his name, "The Lord, He is God." Then in his great triumph on top of Mount Carmel all the people applauded and shouted, "The Lord, He is God." But his real success came at the end of his ministry when he let loose his troops of spiritual geysers to proclaim throughout the nation, "The Lord, He is God."

A Loner to the Last

Before we leave this last story in Elijah's life, we should spend a little time with a couple of problem areas.

The first revolves around the question: Why did Elijah want to get away from Elisha? Three times he told Elisha, "Stay here while I go to the next town," and three times Elisha refused to leave him. But why?

The list of reasons that commentators give is varied:

1. Some say Elijah was testing Elisha to see how strong his faith and resolution were.

2. Others say Elijah wanted to spare Elisha the grief of a final farewell.

3. Still others say Elijah felt so humble and modest about the great event that would soon take place that he didn't think it was right for even Elisha to witness it.

4. And still others say that Elijah thought it would

be best for Elisha to stay with the younger prophets in this time of trauma.

You can take your pick. I think, however, that you might consider a fifth reason. He wanted to be alone. It seems natural to me that Elijah, who was a loner by temperament, would want to spend some time alone before he met God face to face.

No matter what reason Elijah had for his request, Elisha stuck with him, as Ruth stayed with Naomi. No matter what Elijah's reasons were, the incident proved Elisha's faithfulness.

It is not easy to play second fiddle. Elisha lived many years in the shadow of Elijah and during those years he apparently didn't receive the honor or respect he deserved from the sons of the prophets. Nevertheless, Elisha remained faithful in his behind-the-scenes role. He was thought of as Elijah's servant rather than as a prophet in his own right. He was known as the man who poured water on the hands of Elijah (2 Kings 3:11). Despite the fact that he was the son of a wealthy farmer, accustomed to the finer things in life, he resolved to be Elijah's faithful servant to the last.

A Double Portion

There's another problem area in this passage. This concerns the "double portion" that Elisha requested of his master. At first glance it looks as if Elisha was getting greedy. As the song goes, "Anything you can do, I can do better." It looks as if Elisha wanted to be twice as successful as Elijah in everything. It appears to be gross one-upmanship. But that is not the case.

The "double portion of his spirit" is a reference to Deuteronomy 21:17, where the firstborn son in receiving his inheritance to carry on the family name was given a double portion. Elisha wanted to be acknowledged as Elijah's spiritual heir, equipped to serve God in a way that would befit the memory of Elijah.

Far from being grasping, Elisha's request for a double portion shows his humility. It reveals his incapability of carrying on Elijah's ministry in his own talent and strength.

Though he had been trained for years at Elijah's side, he still felt he needed all the help he could get to be worthy of being Elijah's successor. Just as Joshua needed divine encouragement (Josh. 1) after he had been named Moses' successor, so Elisha needed encouragement to succeed Elijah.

While Elijah could treat Elisha as a son, he couldn't really make him a prophet. That was something that God would have to do. Hence, Elijah's rather ambiguous reply to Elisha's request.

In the final event in Elijah's life, he was taken to heaven in a whirlwind. He thus became one of two Bible characters who did not actually die. The other, of course, was the Patriarch Enoch, who "walked with God and was not, for God took him" (Gen. 5:24, KJV). Both of these stories are shrouded in mystery and it is best not to make more nor less of them than the Bible does.

Another story shrouded in mystery is of the death of Moses who, according to Scripture, was buried by God in the land of Moab (Deut. 34:6). No more details are given.

Interestingly enough, it was Elijah and Moses who reappeared in person on the Mount of Transfiguration to talk with Christ about His impending death. Many scholars identify Elijah and Moses as the two witnesses who will return to earth (Rev. 11). The prophet

Malachi named Elijah as one who would be sent "before the coming of the great and terrible Day of the Lord" (Mal. 4:5).

Strange, isn't it, that all this should happen to Elijah, who "was a man with a nature like ours." He hadn't lived a life of perfection. His name doesn't appear in the great chapter on faith, Hebrews 11. But God remembered him. It may be because his life was open before God, so transparent to men, that he was given as an example to us. Only one recorded prayer of Elijah's was never answered by God. And that prayer was that God would take his life.

What a way to go!